ANGOLA

ANGOLA

1880 TO THE PRESENT:
SLAVERY, EXPLOITATION, AND REVOLT

BRUCE AND BECKY DUROST FISH

INTRODUCTORY ESSAY BY
Dr. Richard E. Leakey
Chairman, Wildlife Clubs
of Kenya Association
·┼·
AFTERWORD BY
Deirdre Shields

CHELSEA HOUSE PUBLISHERS
Philadelphia
In association with Covos Day Books, South Africa

CHELSEA HOUSE PUBLISHERS

EDITOR IN CHIEF Sally Cheney
ASSOCIATE EDITOR IN CHIEF Kim Shinners
ART DIRECTOR Sara Davis
ASSOCIATE ART DIRECTOR Takeshi Takahashi
SERIES DESIGNER Keith Trego
COVER DESIGN Emiliano Begnardi

The Chelsea House World Wide Web address is http://www.chelseahouse.com
First Printing
1 3 5 7 9 8 6 4 2

Library of Congress Cataloging-in-Publication Data

Fish, Bruce.
   Angola, 1880 to the present : slavery, exploitation, and revolt / Bruce and Becky Durost
Fish ; introductory essay by Richard E. Leakey ; afterword by Deirdre Shields.
      p. cm.-- (Exploration of Africa, the emerging nations)
   Includes bibliographical references and index.
   Summary: Photographs and text look at the past, development, and present culture of
Angola and its inhabitants.
   ISBN 0-7910-6197-3 (alk. paper)
   1. Angola—History—Juvenile literature. [1. Angola.] I. Fish, Becky Durost. II. Title. III.
Series.

DT1325 .F57 2001
920.72'0978--dc21

                                                                    2001042455

The photographs in this book are from the Royal Geographical Society Picture Library. Most are being published for the first time.

The Royal Geographical Society Picture Library provides an unrivaled source of over half a million images of peoples and landscapes from around the globe. Photographs date from the 1840s onwards on a variety of subjects including the British Colonial Empire, deserts, exploration, indigenous peoples, landscapes, remote destinations, and travel.

Photography, beginning with the daguerreotype in 1839, is only marginally younger than the Society, which encouraged its explorers to use the new medium from its earliest days. From the remarkable mid-19th century black-and-white photographs to color transparencies of the late 20th century, the focus of the collection is not the generic stock shot but the portrayal of man's resilience, adaptability, and mobility in remote parts of the world.

In organizing this project, we have incurred many debts of gratitude. Our first, though, is to the professional staff of the Picture Library for their generous assistance, especially to Joanna Scadden, Picture Library Manager.

CONTENTS

Exploration of Africa: The Emerging Nations

THE DARK CONTINENT

DR. RICHARD E. LEAKEY

THE CONCEPT OF AFRICAN exploration has been greatly influenced by the hero status given to the European adventurers and missionaries who went off to Africa in the last century. Their travels and travails were certainly extraordinary and nobody can help but be impressed by the tremendous physical and intellectual courage that was so much a characteristic of people such as Livingstone, Stanley, Speke, and Baker, to name just a few. The challenges and rewards that Africa offered, both in terms of commerce and also "saved souls," inspired people to take incredible risks and endure personal suffering to a degree that was probably unique to the exploration of Africa.

I myself was fortunate enough to have had the opportunity to organize one or two minor expeditions to remote spots in Africa where there were no roads or airfields and marching with porters and/or camels was the best option at the time. I have also had the thrill of being with people untouched and often unmoved by contact with Western or other technologically based cultures, and these experiences remain for me amongst the most exciting and salutary of my life. With the contemporary revolution in technology, there will be few if any such opportunities again. Indeed I often find myself slightly saddened by the realization that were life ever discovered on another planet, exploration would doubtless be done by remote sensing and making full use of artificial, digital intelligence. At least it is unlikely to be in my lifetime and this is a relief!

Notwithstanding all of this, I believe that the age of exploration and discovery in Africa is far from over. The future offers incredible opportunities for new discoveries that will push back the frontiers of knowledge. This endeavor will of course not involve exotic and arduous journeys into malaria-infested tropical swamps, but it will certainly require dedication, team work, public support, and a conviction that the rewards to be gained will more than justify the efforts and investment.

Early Explorers

Many of us were raised and educated at school with the belief that Africa, the so-called Dark Continent, was actually discovered by early European travelers and explorers. The date of this "discovery" is difficult to establish, and anyway a distinction has always had to be drawn between northern Africa and the vast area south of the Sahara. The Romans certainly had information about the continent's interior as did others such as the Greeks. A diverse range of traders ventured down both the west coast and the east coast from at least the ninth century, and by the tenth century Islam had taken root in a number of new towns and settlements established by Persian and Arab interests along the eastern tropical shores. Trans-African trade was probably under way well before this time, perhaps partly stimulated by external interests.

Close to the beginning of the first millennium, early Christians were establishing the Coptic church in the ancient kingdom of Ethiopia and at other coastal settlements along Africa's northern Mediterranean coast. Along the west coast of Africa, European trade in gold, ivory, and people was well established by the sixteenth century. Several hundred years later, early in the 19th century, the systematic penetration and geographical exploration of Africa was undertaken by Europeans seeking geographical knowledge and territory and looking for opportunities not only for commerce but for the chance to spread the Gospel. The extraordinary narratives of some of the journeys of early European travelers and adventurers in Africa are a vivid reminder of just how recently Africa has become embroiled in the power struggles and vested interests of non-Africans.

THE DARK CONTINENT

AFRICA'S GIFT TO THE WORLD

My own preoccupation over the past thirty years has been to study human prehistory, and from this perspective it is very clear that Africa was never "discovered" in the sense in which so many people have been and, perhaps, still are being taught. Rather, it was Africans themselves who found that there was a world beyond their shores.

Prior to about two million years ago, the only humans or proto-humans in existence were confined to Africa; as yet, the remaining world had not been exposed to this strange mammalian species, which in time came to dominate the entire planet. It is no trivial matter to recognize the cultural implications that arise from this entirely different perspective of Africa and its relationship to the rest of humanity.

How many of the world's population grow up knowing that it was in fact African people who first moved and settled in southern Europe and Central Asia and migrated to the Far East? How many know that Africa's principal contribution to the world is in fact humanity itself? These concepts are quite different from the notion that Africa was only "discovered" in the past few hundred years and will surely change the commonly held idea that somehow Africa is a "laggard," late to come onto the world stage.

It could be argued that our early human forebears—the *Homo erectus* who moved out of Africa—have little or no bearing on the contemporary world and its problems. I disagree and believe that the often pejorative thoughts that are associated with the Dark Continent and dark skins, as well as with the general sense that Africans are somehow outside the mainstream of human achievement, would be entirely negated by the full acceptance of a universal African heritage for all of humanity. This, after all, is the truth that has now been firmly established by scientific inquiry.

The study of human origins and prehistory will surely continue to be important in a number of regions of Africa and this research must continue to rank high on the list of relevant ongoing exploration and discovery. There is still much to be learned about the early stages of human development, and the age of the "first humans"—the first bipedal apes—has not been firmly established. The current hypothesis is that prior to five million years ago there were no bipeds, and this would mean that humankind is only five million years old. Beyond Africa, there were no humans until just two million years ago, and this is a consideration that political leaders and people as a whole need to bear in mind.

RECENT HISTORY

When it comes to the relatively recent history of Africa's contemporary people, there is still considerable ignorance. The evidence suggests that there were major migrations of people within the continent during the past 5,000 years, and the impact of the introduction of domestic stock must have been quite considerable on the way of life of many of Africa's people. Early settlements and the beginnings of nation states are, as yet, poorly researched and recorded. Although archaeological studies have been undertaken in Africa for well over a hundred years, there remain more questions than answers.

One question of universal interest concerns the origin and inspiration for the civilization of early Egypt. The Nile has, of course, offered opportunities for contacts between the heart of Africa and the Mediterranean seacoast, but very little is known about human settlement and civilization in the upper reaches of the Blue and White Nile between 4,000 and 10,000 years ago. We do know that the present Sahara Desert is only about 10,000 years old; before this Central Africa was wetter and more fertile, and research findings have shown that it was only during the past 10,000 years that Lake Turkana in the northern Kenya was isolated from the Nile system. When connected, it would have been an excellent connection between the heartland of the continent and the Mediterranean.

Another question focuses on the extensive stone-walled villages and towns in Southern Africa. The Great Zimbabwe is but one of thousands of standing monuments in East, Central, and Southern Africa that attest to considerable human endeavor in Africa long before contact with Europe or Arabia. The Neolithic period and Iron Age still offer very great opportunities for exploration and discovery.

As an example of the importance of history, let us look at the modern South Africa where a visitor might still be struck by the not-too-subtle representation of a past that, until a few years ago, only "began" with the arrival of Dutch settlers some 400 years back. There are, of course, many pre-Dutch sites, including extensive fortified towns where kingdoms and nation states had thrived hundreds of years before contact with Europe; but this evidence has been poorly documented and even more poorly portrayed.

Few need to be reminded of the sparseness of Africa's precolonial written history. There are countless cultures and historical narratives that have been recorded only as oral history and legend. As postcolonial Africa further consolidates itself, history must be reviewed and deepened to incorporate the realities of precolonial human settlement as well as foreign contact. Africa's identity and self-respect is closely linked to this.

One of the great tragedies is that African history was of little interest to the early European travelers who were in a hurry and had no brief to document the details of the people they came across during their travels. In the basements of countless European museums, there are stacked shelves of African "curios"—objects taken from the people but seldom documented in terms of the objects' use, customs, and history.

There is surely an opportunity here for contemporary scholars to do something. While much of Africa's precolonial past has been obscured by the slave trade, colonialism, evangelism, and modernization, there remains an opportunity, at least in some parts of the continent, to record what still exists. This has to be one of the most vital frontiers for African exploration and discovery as we approach the end of this millennium. Some of the work will require trips to the field, but great gains could be achieved by a systematic and coordinated effort to record the inventories of European museums and archives. The Royal Geographical Society could well play a leading role in this chapter of African exploration. The compilation of a central data bank on what is known and what exists would, if based on a coordinated initiative to record the customs and social organization of Africa's remaining indigenous peoples, be a huge contribution to the heritage of humankind.

Medicines and Foods

On the African continent itself, there remain countless other areas for exploration and discovery. Such endeavors will be achieved without the fanfare of great expeditions and high adventure as was the case during the last century and they should, as far as possible, involve exploration and discovery of African frontiers by Africans themselves. These frontiers are not geographic: they are boundaries of knowledge in the sphere of Africa's home-grown cultures and natural world.

Indigenous knowledge is a very poorly documented subject in many parts of the world, and Africa is a prime example of a continent where centuries of accumulated local knowledge is rapidly disappearing in the face of modernization. I believe, for example, that there is much to be learned about the use of wild African plants for both medicinal and nutritional purposes. Such knowledge, kept to a large extent as the experience and memory of elders in various indigenous communities, could potentially have far-reaching benefits for Africa and for humanity as a whole.

The importance of new remedies based on age-old medicines cannot be underestimated. Over the past two decades, international companies have begun to take note and to exploit certain African plants for pharmacological preparations. All too often, Africa has not been the beneficiary of these "discoveries," which are, in most instances, nothing more than the refinement and improvement of traditional African medicine. The opportunities for exploration and discovery in this area are immense and will have assured economic return on investment. One can only hope that such work will be in partnership with the people of Africa and not at the expense of the continent's best interests.

Within the same context, there is much to be learned about the traditional knowledge of the thousands of plants that have been utilized by different African communities for food. The contemporary world has become almost entirely dependent, in terms of staple foods, on the cultivation of only six principal plants: corn, wheat, rice, yams, potatoes, and bananas. This cannot be a secure basis to guarantee the food requirements of more than five billion people.

Many traditional food plants in Africa are drought resistant and might well offer new alternatives for large-scale agricultural development in the years to come. Crucial to this development is finding out what African people used before exotics were introduced. In some rural areas of the continent, it is still possible to learn about much of this by talking to the older generation. It is certainly a great shame that some of the early European travelers in Africa were ill equipped to study and record details of diet and traditional plant use, but I am sure that, although it is late, it is not too late. The compilation of a pan-African database on what is known about the use of the continent's plant resources is a vital matter requiring action.

Vanishing Species

In the same spirit, there is as yet a very incomplete inventory of the continent's other species. The inevitable trend of bringing land into productive management is resulting in the loss of unknown but undoubtedly large numbers of species. This genetic resource may be invaluable to the future of Africa and indeed humankind, and there really is a need for coordinated efforts to record and understand the continent's biodiversity.

In recent years important advances have been made in the study of tropical ecosystems in Central and South America, and I am sure that similar endeavors in Africa would be rewarding. At present, Africa's semi-arid and highland ecosystems are better understood than the more diverse and complex lowland forests, which are themselves under particular threat from loggers and farmers. The challenges of exploring the biodiversity of the upper canopy in the tropical forests, using the same techniques that are now used in Central American forests, are fantastic and might also lead to eco-tourist developments for these areas in the future.

It is indeed an irony that huge amounts of money are being spent by the advanced nations in an effort to discover life beyond our own planet, while at the same time nobody on this planet knows the extent and variety of life here at home. The tropics are especially relevant in this regard and one can only hope that Africa will become the focus of renewed efforts of research on biodiversity and tropical ecology.

An Afrocentric View

Overall, the history of Africa has been presented from an entirely Eurocentric or even Caucasocentric perspective, and until recently this has not been adequately reviewed. The penetration of Africa, especially during the last century, was important in its own way; but today the realities of African history, art, culture, and politics are better known. The time has come to regard African history in terms of what has happened in Africa itself, rather than simply in terms of what non-African individuals did when they first traveled to the continent.

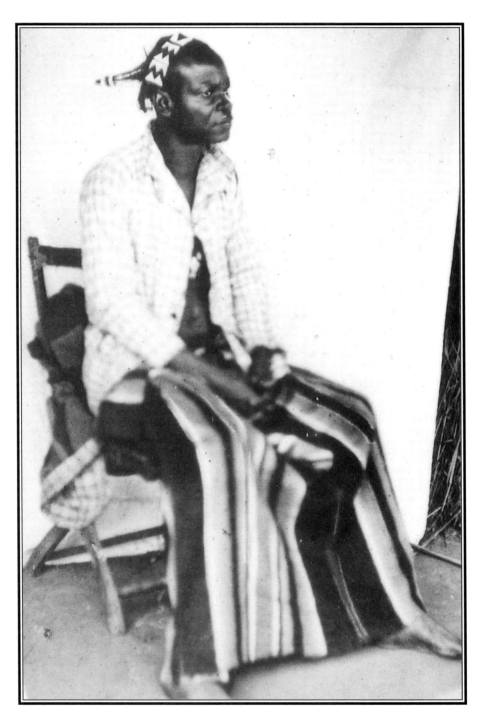

Lunda Man in Full Dress, c. 1890

1

THE TRADER

The 73-year-old man shook his head. He was angry and sad, but most of all he was tired. For 50 years he had dedicated himself to increasing the power and wealth of his homeland, Portugal, and to improving the lives of the Africans with whom he lived. But in 1890 one thing was abundantly clear to António Francisco da Silva Porto: stubbornness and pride on the part of both Europeans and Africans were about to create a violent confrontation. And he seemed unable to prevent it. His friends and neighbors would suffer, and his homeland would once again look weak and foolish. The British, the French, the Germans, and even the Belgians would have one more reason to ignore the Portuguese as they divided Africa among themselves.

Many believed that Silva Porto was the most influential person in central Angola, but the events of the past few weeks had confirmed his own suspicions of recent years that his authority was fading. He had failed to convince either Ndunduma, the ***soba*** (ruler) of the Viye Kingdom, or Portuguese Captain Paiva Couceiro to set aside their demands and accept a compromise solution to their conflict. Couceiro was determined to lead his soldiers across territory claimed by the prosperous kingdom, and Ndunduma absolutely refused them permission to enter his realm.

A Group of Lunda Dancers, 1890

The old Portuguese trader and explorer examined the situation one more time. Only a dramatic gesture would shock both leaders enough to force them to reconsider their actions. With sudden determination, Silva Porto walked quickly to his house and began dragging kegs of gunpowder into one of its rooms.

Like his life, his death would be dramatic—an end no one in the northern coastal city of Porto, Portugal, would have imagined for the son of a poverty-stricken family named Silva. Even though no money had been available for a proper education, their son had heard many stories about adventures at sea and in far-off colonies. Portuguese sailors had been the first Europeans to venture south in the Atlantic Ocean beyond the equator in the 1400s. They had been pioneers in establishing trade routes along the Western African coast and across the Atlantic to South America. In 1487 Bartolomeu Dias was the

Lunda Man, Showing Hairdressing, c. 1890 *The Lunda are a Bantu-speaking people who are part of the Lunda-Chokwe group. As the hyphenation implies, this category comprises at least two peoples, the origins of which are known to be different, although historic events brought them together as one group. The Lunda alone were part of the Lunda Empire (seventeenth to nineteenth centuries) in the present northeastern part of Angola.*

The photographs of the Lunda shown in this book were taken by Henrique de Carvalho (1843–1909).

first European to round the Cape of Good Hope at the southern tip of Africa, opening a new route to the riches of India and the Far East.

The Portuguese still dreamed of a worldwide empire, but in the nineteenth century political and economic instability blocked their path. To achieve a prosperous and secure future, they believed that the commercial contacts and colonial possessions already established in South America, Africa, India, and the Far East had to be developed. Silva Porto grew up in a world filled with the promise of Portuguese civilization.

Seeking Adventure

When he turned 12 years old in 1829, António da Silva was expected to become an apprentice and learn a trade. Eager for adventure, he took a ship to Rio de Janeiro, Brazil. Working both in Rio and in the town of Bahia, he was trained as a merchant. Brazil was known for its huge coffee plantations where slaves worked long hours and generated huge profits. Most of these slaves came from West Africa, particularly from Angola. So Silva, who added Porto to his name in honor of his home town, learned about the slave trade as well as trade in coffee and other commodities.

After 10 years of training, Silva Porto took a ship from Brazil to Luanda, the capital city of Angola. Located where the Kwanza River empties into the Atlantic Ocean, Luanda had been the most

Lunda Woman with Children, c. 1890

Cuanhama, 1890 *The Cuanhama people were part of the ethnolinguistic Ambro group. They lived in the southern part of Angola near the Namibia border. This photograph is of the son and grandson of the Cuanhama chief. It can be assumed that the older man had converted to Christianity. Most probably, this was a recent conversion, as the photographer, Henrique de Carvalho, a noted Portuguese explorer, mapped this area in 1889–1890. A Catholic priest accompanied Carvalho.*

important port on the West African coast for shipping slaves to Europe and the Americas. Although exact figures are difficult to calculate, most scholars agree that approximately 13 million slaves arrived in various parts of the Americas between 1500 and 1850. Of those, 4 million came from Angola, making it the largest single source of slaves in the world.

By 1839, when Silva Porto arrived, slavery was changing. In 1807 the British Empire, which accounted for half the worldwide demand for slaves, made importing slaves to the British Isles or any of its colonies illegal. However, the ownership of the slaves already present throughout the Empire remained legal for some time. The United States and other European nations soon followed Britain's lead and made the commercial traffic in slaves, but not slavery itself, illegal. Just three years before Silva Porto reached Africa, Portugal also adopted this policy. Nevertheless, the illegal movement of slaves across the Atlantic continued, because Angola had stronger economic and religious ties with Brazil than it did with the Portuguese government. Silva Porto and most other Portuguese in Angola continued to own slaves and considered slavery a necessary tool for the economic development of Africa.

During the next two years, Silva Porto traded in the back country around Luanda. He became one of many **pombeiros,** a name given originally to merchants who controlled the two major slave-gathering routes in Angola. After the slave trade became illegal, *pombeiro* became a more general term for all traders in Angola. Silva Porto observed how the traffic in human beings was gradually being replaced by transactions involving ivory, coffee, cotton, wax, rum, and other products. Then he moved south to the coastal city of Benguela. This gave him more direct access to the ivory trade in southern Angola, which was becoming quite lucrative because the Portuguese monarchy no longer had a monopoly on it.

São Miguel Fortress, 1899 *Entering Luanda Harbor. The Portugese began construction on this fortress in the mid-seventeenth century.*

Mataba Chief, 1890 *The Mataba belonged to the Lunda-Chokwe group. They lived in the northeastern part of Angola. In the hyphenated name of this ethnolinguistic group, "Lunda" refers to the great empire of Central Africa, which extended into Angola in the seventeenth century. By the end of the nineteenth century, the Mataba, and their fellow Chokwe allies, had established an independent "mini" economic domain stretching from central Angola eastward to the Congo border. They controlled a thriving trade in ivory, beeswax, and rubber. In their trading, they had accumulated firearms and were skilled hunters. By trade or raid, the Chokwe acquired many women slaves of child-bearing age, which greatly added to their population. David Livingstone, the Scottish missionary and explorer who crossed the Chokwe lands in the 1850s, described them as the most savage and least hospitable people he had met.*

As the years passed, Silva Porto became wealthy and influential, but he never lost his desire for adventure. By 1845 he had established a trading post 390 miles from the coast in the center of the Viye Kingdom (which the Portuguese called Bié).

Caminho de Ferro de Luanda, 1899 *The Caminho de Ferro Luanda railroad began operation in 1899, when it reached Ambaca, 173 miles from Luanda. When completed, the railroad covered a total of 378 miles, its main line running from Luanda to Malanje, with two spurs to Dondo on the Kwanza River and to the Golunga Alto coffee area. Railroad construction was essential to the Angolan economy. Portuguese expansionists envisioned a trans-African railroad linking Mozambique, their colony in East Africa, with Angola. However, because of financial restraints, this grandiose scheme never reached fruition. In fact, until the mid-1920s, most Angolan settlers had to transport their agricultural produce from the interior by expensive ox-carts or African porters.*

Portugese Merchant, c. 1876
Trade was the main economic preoccupation of the Portugese in Angola. They exported slaves to enrich Brazilian plantations rather than developing large-scale farming in Angola itself. While coffee and sugar plantations date back to the 1830's, the importance of plantation agriculture in Angola is essentially a post-World War-II phenomenon.

There he built a home and stockade, which he named Belmonte. From this center, he managed the trade of slaves, ivory, and other products.

Eventually, Silva Porto married a woman from a prominent Viye family. The Viye were one of several kingdoms that made up the Ovimbundu people. During the 1800s, the Ovimbundu became the most important African traders in the southern half of the continent. Silva Porto's family ties to these people helped to increase his business opportunities, and they in turn were pleased to strengthen their connection with European merchants. Silva Porto was treated by them like a member of the ruling class.

Over the years, he painstakingly explored the surrounding area, earning himself the title of ***sertanejo*** or backwoodsman. He created a new trade route and became the confidant of many area rulers. In 1852 Swahili traders from the eastern coast of Africa

Joaquim Cordeiro, c. 1880 *The journalist Joaquim Dias Cordeiro da Matta (1857–1894) was one of the very few assimilated intellectuals in Luanda who spoke out against the abuses of Portuguese colonialism while reaffirming his Angolan identity. Cordeiro supported an Angolan autochthonous or native culture. He collected local proverbs and sayings* (Filosofia Popular em Provérbsios Angoleneses, 1891).

After the collapse of the Portuguese monarchy in 1910 and the advent of the Republican government in Lisbon, the assimilados, *as the anticolonialists were known, formed the Liga Angolana in Luanda. This small group, mainly made up of civil servants, lacked a substantial following and had extremely limited influence in changing Portuguese rule in Angola. But, this group is important historically because it was the first to advocate an independent Angola—and Cordeiro can be considered the founder of this movement.*

Antonio Moreira, C. 1876
The 1870's and 1880's saw the emergence of a small group of educated second generation Potugese-Angolans who considered themselves Angolans. Moreira was a member of this group who studied the history, language and legends of the indigenous Angolan peoples. His followers in both Luanda and Lisbon published a virulently anticolonial tract entitled Voz d'Angola clamando no deserto *(1901).*

arrived in Benguela, and the provincial governor of Angola asked Silva Porto to return with them carrying a message for the governor of Mozambique, another Portuguese colony.

Before the year was out, Silva Porto began the return journey with the help of several African slaves and servants, who carried supplies and weapons. When the terrain became very rough, they even carried Silva Porto himself. Heavy rains and local wars slowed the already difficult journey. By the time the party reached Barotseland, halfway across the continent, Silva Porto was quite ill. While he was recovering, news reached him that the local rulers in the territories lying ahead would not allow a white man to cross their land. In response to this threat, he asked some of his African *pombeiros* to complete the journey. One of

them, Domingos Cakahanga, kept a diary of the trip that was later edited by Silva Porto and published.

A NEW MISSION

Although Silva Porto was disappointed that he had to remain in Barotseland, his stay there allowed him to meet the British explorer and missionary David Livingstone, who was traveling across Africa from east to west. Silva Porto advised Livingstone on the best route to follow to reach Luanda, but neither man was particularly impressed by the other. The Portuguese trader concluded that the English missionary was "an inquisitive, somewhat quarrelsome intruder." Livingstone dismissed Silva Porto as a part-African trader, implying that someone of mixed race was somehow inferior. Some experts suggest that the Englishman did this so he could claim to be the first European explorer in that part of Africa.

When Silva Porto parted company with Livingstone, he began a decades-long campaign to convince his government of the absolute necessity of possessing the interior of Angola. In his mind, the arrival of Swahili traders from the east coast along with the presence of the famous Englishman were important warnings. If Portugal limited its development of Angola primarily to the Atlantic Coast, other European powers would be eager to lay claim to its hidden riches. The Benguela Highlands where Silva Porto lived were among the best agricultural lands in southern Africa.

Silva Porto was full of ideas for developing the interior. He advocated building railroads to improve access to trade routes. He wanted more merchants, missionaries, and other Portuguese settlers to move inland. When in 1863 a provincial governor maintained that possession of the coast was all Portugal needed, Silva Porto retorted, "This is how it is in Portugal, where the only things that matter are pointless rivalries, while the foreigner mocks us and even, in his audacity, spits in our faces." His plans were mostly ignored. Portugal did not have the money needed for such expansion, and its citizens were not eager to seek their fortunes in Africa, where diseases killed or crippled most of the Europeans who arrived. Throughout the 1800s the Portuguese made up only about 1 percent of the population of Angola.

Conflict Over Slavery

Developing the interior of Africa was not the only issue on which Silva Porto disagreed with his home country of Portugal. Portugal's growing opposition to slavery incensed the man. When the government in Lisbon gradually began to outlaw slavery in Portugal and her colonies, Silva Porto made this statement:

It is much to be desired that our legislators had limited their patriotic love to the prosperity of the colony and not touched the matter of slavery, letting it continue at home and in the crown colonies, where there might be use for its assistance. Religion, progress, time, and finally, the repression of the traffic to foreign possessions would bring about its extinction; with the advance of civilization slaves and free men would come to be so aware of its benefits that there would be created a love for work. . . . In the absence of this process and with the law of April 29, 1858, the consequences will be the disrespect of the black for white men and, perhaps, assassination will be the final result! Unhappily, the present laws invite such an end.

Like most colonial Portuguese, Silva Porto saw slavery as an economic necessity and worried that its end would bankrupt him. He also felt a paternalistic responsibility for his slaves and treated them in what he considered a humane manner. If punishment was necessary, he used the **palmatorio,** a thick wooden paddle with four to five small holes in it. This device was slapped against the palm of an offender's hand several times, sucking the flesh up through the holes and forming painful welts. Brutal as this sounds, it was much less harsh than the life-threatening beatings with a **chicotte,** a hippopotamus-hide whip that many other slave owners routinely inflicted on their "property." The *chicotte* ripped flesh open and often killed people.

Once again, Silva Porto's views fell on deaf ears. The Portuguese government was under too much internal and external pressure to end slavery. Great Britain had used its warships to intercept slaves bound for Brazil, and Portuguese abolitionists had passed a law in 1869 that made all slaves **libertos.** While they remained answerable to their masters until 1878, the law in theory guaranteed them both pay and protection from physical harm.

Silva Porto thought that releasing his slaves without training them to take care of themselves was more likely to result in death than freedom. He had long believed in the importance of education for all members of society and had sent his own **mestiço** (African-Portuguese) children to school in Portugal. In a sense, he saw his slaves as part of his extended family. Since the government was determined to liberate them, Silva Porto made it his mission to educate them. To that end he began a school at Belmonte to teach the slave children reading skills.

Although the Native Labor Code of 1878 outlawed slavery and appeared to protect the rights of Africans, it actually allowed a new horror to grow in its place. The code contained a vagrancy clause that allowed any "nonproductive" African male to be forced into accepting a labor contract with anyone willing to employ him. The code's definition of vagrancy was so broad that it allowed virtually any African man who was not working

Yombe Carriers, 1907 *The Yombe are a subgroup of the Kongo peoples. These men were employed by a Protestant mission as carriers. Surprisingly, many Angolan missionaries reported a surplus of carriers. A leading Protestant missionary and educator in Angola explained it this way:*

> *As the missionaries arrived in any area they were dependent upon Africans for many services. First they needed carriers to take their baggage from the port to the site chosen as a mission station. Then they needed people to help them clear land, cut down trees, build stick-and-mud houses, cultivate the garden plots, carry water, and gather firewood. To achieve all this required that missionaries learn the local language.*
>
> *As they wrote down new words, the Africans recognized that the white people's magic was a key to his wealth, power, and mysterious communications across oceans and generations, so they wanted to learn to read and write.*

for Europeans or those the Europeans directly controlled to be declared nonproductive and seized for forced labor. To no one's surprise, it was soon discovered that the labor contracts of former slaves could be sold just as easily as the slaves themselves.

Silva Porto was able to keep control of his slaves, but other forces were conspiring to drive him toward bankruptcy. In the 1880s Portugal finally began to expand its commercial activities into the Angolan interior, but the new companies were less willing to pay taxes to local rulers. This cut their costs and allowed them to undersell established traders.

**Central Angolan Village,
1896**

In 1885 Silva Porto accepted a job as captain major in Bié. As a government employee he was less dependent on income from trade, and his years of experience made him a perfect intermediary between Europeans and the various Ovimbundu kingdoms. He often helped Europeans adjust to their new environment. During a period of local conflict in 1884, he escorted Scottish missionary Frederick Stanley Arnot to the relative safety of Bié. Arnot's journals record the missionary's insistence that he ride an ox rather than be carried in a hammock by African porters. During one 24-hour period, Arnot singed his eye while repairing a breechloader, lost his riding ox, and marched ten miles through knee-high water and rough brush. Silva Porto himself lost the sight in one eye because of an infection. These experiences were typical of the hardships presented by travel and disease in Angola.

The End of an Era

As Silva Porto approached his mid-seventies, he could tell that two centuries of relatively peaceful coexistence between the Ovimbundu and the Portuguese were coming to an end. Internal conflict among the ruling classes of the Ovimbundu weakened the member kingdoms just when the Portuguese government was becoming more committed to occupying the interior of Angola.

In 1888 Ndunduma became head of the Viye Kingdom. He was outspoken in his criticism of the Portuguese, and he publicly accused Silva Porto of betraying African interests. Silva Porto ignored his insults and remained a vital link between the two very different worlds. Near the end of 1889, he took part in lengthy negotiations between Ndunduma and the Scottish missionary Arnot that allowed the missionary to travel through Viye territory.

It was to be Silva Porto's last triumph. Early in 1890 a Portuguese military force of 150 entered Viye. Ndunduma ordered the expedition to withdraw. Couceiro refused and sent the old trader to Ndunduma with orders to change his mind. The *soba* was incensed that the soldiers would send an emissary rather than appearing in person, considering this a calculated insult to his authority. In spite of Silva Porto's insistence that he would be wise to simply let the party pass through his land, Ndunduma again refused.

Silva Porto could see nothing but disaster ahead. He went to his home in Belmonte, wrapped himself in a Portuguese flag, and stretched out on top of at least a dozen kegs of gunpowder, which he then ignited. The resulting explosion left him alive, but severely burned. Both Couceiro and Dr. Fisher, a member of Arnot's missionary group, tried to save the man, but he died the next day.

The soldiers temporarily withdrew from the area, but later in the year a stronger military force returned to Viye, defeated the *soba,* and exiled him to the Cape Verde Islands. As Silva Porto had feared, life for both the Portuguese and the Ovimbundu had been changed forever.

Lunda Drums, c. 1890

2

THE ARISTOCRAT

While Silva Porto was despairing of life, a much younger Portuguese man brimmed with confidence about the future. But because he also refused to admit his own mistakes, Major Alexandre Alberto da Rocha, Visconde de Serpa Pinto, stood on the brink of creating an international crisis.

As his name indicated, Serpa Pinto was a member of the Portuguese aristocracy. In vivid contrast to Silva Porto's humble beginnings, Serpa Pinto was born on April 20, 1846 at Castle Polchras on the Douro River in northern Portugal. At age 12 he entered Portugal's military college, and by 1864 he was an officer serving with a cavalry unit in the army. Five years later, his unit was one of several sent to subdue a rebellion among Africans near the lower Zambezi River who were objecting to European control of their land. What he saw and experienced fired his imagination. Over the next few years Serpa Pinto worked to advance his military career and achieved the rank of major, but he could not forget Africa. The young aristocrat constantly searched for ways to return to the vast continent.

Such opportunities were rare, because Portugal usually ignored her colonies and trading partners unless trouble erupted. But that attitude changed in 1876, when the International Geographical Conference was held in Brussels, Belgium—and Portugal was not invited to participate. The Portuguese were deeply offended. Had they not been the first Europeans to open the Atlantic to navigation? Were they not the first to chart the vast extent of the western and eastern coasts of the African continent? Was it not their naval explorers who had created the Age of Discovery, that great outburst of exploration and conquest that had shaped world history for 400 years?

Of course, Portugal had not been a major power in Europe for the last 300 years, but that point was easily forgotten. They were still the true heirs of Prince Henry the Navigator.

EXPLORING AFRICA

Fueled by a passion to prove to the world that a terrible wrong had been done to them, the Geographical Society of Lisbon funded an expedition to explore the land between Portugal's largest colonies in Africa: Angola on the west coast, and Mozambique on the east coast. The expedition would also survey the watershed between the basins of the Congo and Zambezi Rivers. One small fact was easily obscured in the frantic preparations that followed: the Geographical Society of Lisbon had been founded in 1875, and this was its first major expedition.

The society chose a young naval officer with African experience, Lieutenant Hermenigildo Capelo, to head the expedition, which was scheduled to leave Portugal in 1877. When Serpa Pinto heard the news, he used all his influence to arrange an immediate meeting with Capelo and then overwhelmed the younger man with tales of his previous adventures in Africa. Duly impressed, Capelo welcomed Serpa Pinto's involvement and even invited him along on trips to purchase equipment in Paris and London. Capelo did not yet realize that Major Serpa Pinto was quite adept at exaggerating his own abilities and stealing credit for other people's accomplishments.

In July 1877 the expedition set out for Luanda, Angola. Capelo was the expedition's meteorologist and natural scientist. Serpa Pinto was personnel officer, with responsibility for acquiring African porters. Another young naval officer, Lieutenant Roberto Ivens, was the group's topographer; he would map the territory they explored.

Immediately after they arrived in the bustling harbor city that was the seat of Portugal's colonial government in Angola, things began going wrong. Porters were impossible to find. The British explorer Henry Stanley had just emerged at the mouth of the Congo River after discovering its source and mapping many of its tributaries—thus eliminating one of the major tasks the Portuguese expedition had set for itself. Serpa Pinto invited Stanley to meet with them, and the Portuguese party soon understood the grave difficulties they were about to face. Disease, lack of food, and other hardships had stripped 60 pounds from Stanley's already lean frame. Only 116 of the original 356 people in his party had survived the journey.

The Portuguese expedition chose a new goal. They would explore the Cunene River, which started somewhere in central Angola, flowed south, and then turned sharply west, bordering lands claimed by Germany. Serpa Pinto sailed south to the port city of Benguela, hoping for more success in acquiring porters. Weeks later, Capelo and Ivens arrived, and the three changed their minds again. Now they were determined to follow an old slave route directly inland to Bié, where they hoped the trader Silva Porto might assist them. Even with his help, the expedition could not find enough porters.

Serpa Pinto took charge of the search once again, traveling north while Capelo and Ivens remained in the town of Caconda. During the trip, the major became very sick, and it took him weeks to make his way back. In his absence, Capelo and Ivens had found Africans who were willing to help them and had continued on their way. He caught up with the pair at Belmonte, Silva Porto's home, but he was deeply offended by what he perceived as their desertion of him. Later, he claimed that they had abandoned him in a "dangerous and hostile country," an exaggerated description at best.

Bitter arguments erupted over this and many other issues. Serpa Pinto insisted that they should turn east, across the African continent. Capelo, the leader of the expedition, and Ivens wanted to return to their original instructions from Portugal. The three finally decided to split up, and Serpa Pinto, who was still sick, was given a third of the party's equipment. Capelo and Ivens offered to accompany him back to Benguela on the coast, but the major chose to stay at Silva Porto's home while he recovered. The two naval officers continued north beyond Belmonte and eventually made their way back to Luanda, creating the first thorough survey of that area. Serpa Pinto set his eyes to the east.

THE MAJOR'S EXPEDITION

Silva Porto encouraged his guest and promised to support his proposed journey. In late May 1878 the Portuguese army major started east with 23 African porters. By the middle of June, he had crossed the Kwanza River, and on August 24 he reached Lialui, the capital of the Marutse. Though he was following a route familiar to African and Portuguese traders, Serpa Pinto was the first to map it accurately.

He continued east and soon faced new misfortunes. Serpa Pinto claimed afterwards that some of Silva Porto's men attacked his camp on September 6 because the major had been "unceasingly waging war against [Silva Porto's] traffic in slaves." Then Serpa Pinto's porters deserted him, but the king of the Marutse provided the Portuguese explorer with boats so that he could travel down the Zambezi River and reach the camp of the French medical missionary François Coillard.

It is clear from records Serpa Pinto kept during this entire expedition that he was a racist and a man with an exaggerated sense of his own importance, who often blamed others for problems he had created. Silva Porto had already given him a great deal of help, so there is no reason to believe his men were involved in the attack. Other Africans could have been responsible, but since Serpa Pinto's story has never been verified, it is likely he invented the whole incident to hide a conflict with his porters. Serpa Pinto's history of arrogant behavior and racist views makes it is easy to imagine his porters abandoning him after being mistreated once too often. Whatever the truth, when the major arrived at Coillard's camp on October 20, he was once again seriously ill.

The Coillard family nursed Serpa Pinto back to health. Serpa Pinto later described Coillard as "the man who saved [me], and in doing so saved the labours of the expedition which I directed." Early in 1879 the major arrived in Pretoria, South Africa, and from there traveled to Durban on the southeastern coast. On April 19, he returned to Europe and quickly got the record of "his" expedition published.

How I Crossed Africa came out in both Portuguese and English in 1881 and soon appeared in French, German, and Italian as well. All Europe proclaimed Serpa Pinto one of the great heroes of the age. He received many awards from several geographical societies, including the British Royal Geographical Society's Founder's Medal. His fame restored Portuguese pride in its African colonies, and he became a powerful political force who used every available opportunity to encourage the Portuguese people to expand their influence there.

THE BERLIN CONFERENCE

During the winter of 1884–1885, representatives of all the nations of Europe, as well as the United States, gathered in Berlin to settle border disputes arising from the rapid expansion of colonial possessions in Africa. No representatives of African kingdoms or nations were invited to participate. The agenda and deliberations for the meetings were largely controlled by the major colonial powers: Germany, England, France, Belgium, and Portugal. Conference members agreed that a colonial power had to establish "effective occupation" of the lands it was claiming in order to retain the right to possess them. At the time Portugal had direct control over only about 10 percent of Angola, mostly along the coast. Suddenly the nationalist dreams of men like Serpa Pinto and Silva Porto had become an important tool for colonial survival.

But if the dreams of Serpa Pinto served his country well, the self-serving arrogance reflected in his words and actions did not. In April 1886 he stumbled into a diplomatic conflict with the Sultan of Zanzibar, the British, and the Germans. The British minister to Lisbon, G. G. Petre, warned Barros Gomez, the Portuguese minister of foreign affairs, that Serpa Pinto was a firebrand who might embarrass his government. In a letter to another diplomat, he called Serpa Pinto a liar, but conceded that the man's popularity put the Portuguese government in a difficult position: "He is in a way, however, a popular hero and this ostentatious display of vigour under pretext of defending the national interest and honour, thereby causing Portugal to appear as an important Colonial Power to be reckoned with in Africa, flatters the national vanity and no Government here dares run counter to that feeling." Petre would not have been surprised by the telegram Barros Gomez sent to Serpa Pinto after the situation was resolved: "Incident could have had serious results; I approve happy ending, but recommend moderation."

In the years following the Berlin Conference, the government of Portugal faced serious problems in Africa. The earlier decades of the 1800s had seen them survive invasion by French and Spanish forces, civil war, and the loss of their colony Brazil. These events had left Portugal financially weak, politically unstable, and unable to fulfill the grand visions that Serpa Pinto had popularized. And the very limitations that hobbled Portugal made its people even more desperate for a colonial empire that stretched across the African continent, from Angola to Mozambique.

THE BREAK WITH BRITAIN

Matters reached a crisis in 1889. Two Portuguese expeditions left from opposite sides of Africa, planning to meet in the middle of the continent. The one traveling east from Angola became embroiled in the events that led to Silva Porto's suicide. Another group, led by Serpa Pinto, started from Mozambique and traveled west. Their goal was to support Portuguese land claims in the Luangwa River valley and thus block the northward progress of Britain's Cecil Rhodes, who was attempting to establish a line of British possessions from South Africa to Cairo, Egypt.

Serpa Pinto's group included 731 armed men, but he described it as a scientific expedition. He claimed that the soldiers were merely providing protection for engineers who were surveying a route for a future railroad. The local English officials did not believe him, and their suspicions were confirmed when the entire party turned north toward Lake Nyasa. Serpa Pinto had decided to claim the Shire Highlands for Portugal, even though he had been warned to avoid the area. It was inhabited by the Makololo people and had long been under British protection because of their personal ties to Britain's revered missionary and explorer David Livingstone. The Makololo were alarmed to find a large armed force invading their land and soon attacked it, but they were soundly defeated.

Word of the conflict ignited vast public outrage in Britain. The English government complained to Barros Gomes, who insisted that the Portuguese had only been defending themselves. In January 1890 British Lord Salisbury demanded the withdrawal of Portuguese forces and ordered British warships stationed at Zanzibar to steam to Portuguese harbors in Mozambique. Though its claims to the disputed territory were actually stronger than Britain's, Portugal did not have the resources to win a military confrontation with the British Empire. The Portuguese government ordered Serpa Pinto to withdraw and then resigned from office en masse.

It was now the turn of the Portuguese people to be outraged. They had been betrayed by one of their oldest allies and disgraced by the spineless actions of their own government. Demonstrators stoned the house of Barros Gomes, and students in Lisbon swore to die in defense of Portuguese Africa. Private citizens began to raise money to send a cruiser with a squadron of armed men to Mozambique and drive out the British.

Serpa Pinto and others like him had given the people a dream of a Portuguese Africa stretching from coast to coast. They were not yet ready to abandon all hope. But the new Portuguese government understood that the only way to protect the territory it already held in Africa was to begin making compromises with the stronger nations that dominated the map of Europe.

Angolan Dressed in "Feast Robes," 1890 *Henrique de Carvalho, the Portuguese explorer, spent most of the 1880s traveling through remote parts of Angola. He labeled this photograph simply, "Dressed in Feast Robes."*

3

THE TEACHER

People in the port city of Luanda, Angola, paused in the midst of their business on March 20, 1885, to gaze curiously at a group of 45 Americans—29 adults and 16 children—disembarking from a ship in the harbor. Rumors about them had been circulating for weeks, ever since a message had reached the governor-general of Angola from William Taylor, asking for assistance in creating a series of mission stations to serve the interior regions of the country.

Most people in Luanda thought the Methodist bishop was crazy, and they were not alone. An editorial in the *New York Times* summed up his work this way:

This is the band led by an alleged Bishop and undoubted crank. . . . He has with him many women and a large number of children, some of whom are mere infants. A madder project than that of marching these women and children into the heart of Africa was never conceived. . . .

Of the forty persons who are to be led into the wilderness by the "crank" in question, it is doubtful if a single one escapes the murderous savages through whom Stanley fought his way on his journey down the Congo. If a remnant does survive to reach the proposed mission field, it is very certain that not one of the women or children will be among them. These helpless people will die like sheep of the deadly coast fever, and the only consolation will be that they will escape the hardship and starvation which must be endured by those who survive. . . .

Luanda Catholic Cathedral, 1899 *Throughout the nineteenth century, the Catholic Church in Portugal suffered a series of severe secular shocks. Every time liberal forces prevailed over the absolute monarchy, the Church declined. The Decree of 1834, for example, abolished all monasteries in Portugal and nationalized their land holdings. A wave of anti-clericalism between 1820 and 1840 greatly reduced the number of priests, from 24,000 to about 10,000. From 1831 to 1873, six dioceses were eliminated.*

The decline of the Catholic Church in Portugal was reflected in Angola. The attrition of the clergy continued during most of the century. The number of Catholic clergy in Angola varied as follows in the 1800s: thirty-nine in 1800, eighteen in 1840, five in 1853, sixteen in 1863, and thirty-eight in 1880.

The five priests in 1853 were all natives of Angola—four were working in two parishes in Luanda and one in the western city of Benguela. Not a single mission was functioning in Angola. A new bishop arriving in Luanda in 1850 found the few clergymen "unfortunately not exemplary," but he could not punish them or he would have been left without any clergy. The result was that most Catholics refused to attend church or receive the sacraments.

The revival of the Catholic Church in Angola was due to a French order, "The Holy Ghost Fathers" or "Spartans." This missionary group took the black people as their special charge, and in January 1887 two Holy Ghost fathers arrived in Luanda to establish a congregation. Later, between 1900 to 1965, Catholic missionaries, encouraged by the Portuguese government, opened 109 new mission stations throughout Angola. The Salazar regime in Portugal, which began in 1926, provided both political and financial assistance to the revived missionary work—and in return, the Church supported Salazar's dictatorial rule.

It would be quite proper to treat them as lunatics and to ship them home by the first vessel. That the leader is a lunatic of a very dangerous kind is evident.

William Taylor, the bishop of Africa for the Methodist Episcopal Church of the United States, was a controversial figure. He wanted to change the way Christian missions operated, and no one doubted he would do everything in his power to make his dreams a reality.

MISSIONS IN ANGOLIA

Christianity had first come to Angola 400 years earlier, with the arrival of Portuguese Roman Catholic priests who had been invited by African kings. But over the years, many priests had been corrupted by the wealth and power they could accumulate through the slave trade. Some were forced to return to Portugal by African rulers who grew tired of seeing their people abused. In the last hundred years, political turmoil in Portugal had also diminished the presence of Roman Catholicism in Angola. In 1853, only five Roman Catholic clergy remained in the entire colony, and their reputations were so bad that people refused to attend mass.

This situation began to change dramatically during the last decades of the nineteenth century, when the Congregation of the Holy Ghost first appeared in Angola and began to slowly rebuild the Roman Catholic Church. This French order, popularly known as the Holy Ghost Fathers, operated under the authority of the Vatican, but also entered into an agreement with Portugal. The document that defined this arrangement was called the **Padroado.** It gave the Portuguese king control over the appointment of bishops and missionaries for Angola and also allowed him to create new dioceses, convents, and monasteries. At the same time, it made the Portugese government responsible for funding most of the church's work in the colony by requiring that it provide buildings, supplies, and workers for the missions. Thus the new Roman Catholic work in Angola became an extension of the Portuguese secular government.

Maids with Child, Luanda, 1890 *This Portuguese child is flanked by his Christian maid (left) and her non-Christian counterpart. In 1900 there were less than 9,000 whites living in all of Angola and more than half of these lived in Luanda. Most of the whites were sol-diers or exiled criminals (*degredados*) who had been sent to Angola to serve their sentences rather than being kept in a jail in Portugal. In 1881, of the 1,450 European residents of Luanda, half (721) were civil or military criminals, and only 394 were free men outside of the army. In 1902 there were fewer than 100 European women in Angola, all but eight to ten were* degredados.

Protestant missionaries also began to arrive in the late 1800s. The English Baptists appeared first, focusing their efforts primarily on northernmost Angola along the banks of the Congo River. As other groups arrived, informal agreements over the location of missions kept them from wasteful competition among themselves. Congregationalists from the United States worked with the Ovimbundu in central and southern Angola, while Methodists established missions near the Mbundu in the area around Luanda. Since the Portuguese government had no direct control over the Protestants, it was often suspicious of their activities but generally tolerated them because their presence helped achieve the larger goal of "effective occupation," as required by the Berlin Conference.

UNEXPECTED RECEPTION

Most Protestant missionaries, whether they were Europeans or Americans, were surprised to find that the Africans were not all "heathens," who lacked any knowledge of God. When three Congregationalist missionaries traveled to Bailundo, an Ovimbundu kingdom in central Angola, they were asked to explain their mission to King Ekwikwi II. William Henry Sanders said that they had come to tell the king and his people about God. When the king nodded for Sanders to continue, the American missionary began giving proofs of the existence of God and describing the Ten Commandments. "Stop!"

The São Salvador School, 1907 *Two students are standing in front of the school building on the left in this photograph of the Reverend Thomas Lewis's mission. It seems that the two boys in the center were out food gathering. Lewis labeled this image, "A step in civilization!"*

Although his main mission was in São Salvador, Lewis traveled throughout the Kongo region, which is the northern province of Angola. São Salvador, a tiny town that does not appear on most maps, had been the capital of the ancient Kongo Kingdom. Then called M'banza Congo, it was renamed by the Portuguese for a long since destroyed cathedral that was built there in 1534. The town's original name was restored after Angola obtained its independence from Portugal in 1975.

Ekwikwi shouted. "If that is all you've come to tell us, you can go home because we know that already!"

Nor did they expect to have their methods openly and intelligently challenged by local rulers. After the first Baptist missionaries had been at São Salvador, the ancient capital of the Kongo Kingdom in northern Angola, for several weeks, the king called for them. "I do not understand the way in which you are behaving," he said. "You told me that you had come to teach me and my people about God, and yet you do not do so. You have been here four Sundays. You gather together on Sunday and read, and sing, and pray, but you never ask me or anyone else to join you; you never teach us. What sort of missionaries are you? You must teach us. This will not do at all."

The missionaries insisted that they could not yet speak the local language fluently, but the king brushed aside their excuse. "Fluently! You can ask me for things you want, carriers and so forth, and conduct any business that you may have; you know quite enough to begin to teach us; at any rate you must try." The next Sunday, the missionaries held a service for everyone, with the assistance of an escaped slave named Misilina, who spoke a language similar to Kikongo. With the king's encouragement, the services soon became a regular part of life in São Salvador.

Many members of all the mission groups died from tropical diseases such as yellow fever and malaria. The first four missionaries sent to Angola by the Holy Ghost Fathers died within four years of their arrival. The Baptists were plagued with illness from the moment they arrived at São Salvador, losing their leader's wife by the end of the first month. The first head of the Congregationalist work died less than a year after reaching Bailundo.

Suspicions about the motives of the white missionaries had to be overcome as well. When Walter T. Currie, a Canadian missionary, arrived in Chissamba, his presence raised many questions. Even though he traveled with African helpers, people were afraid of this lone white man and carefully avoided him. Finally an elder had his two sons spend the night with Currie. Kumba, one of the boys, said, "I slept with one eye open and both ears. I wasn't sure of the white man. Father

Street Scene, Luanda, 1899

bade me go. I obeyed. But my uncle said to me as I left our home village, 'White men eat boys.' I trembled. Morning light came. I was uneaten. The dawn was gladsome."

The Holy Ghost Fathers faced a more serious situation. After they arrived in Cabinda, along the coast just north of the Congo River, the seasonal rains failed, a plague of fleas appeared, and a smallpox epidemic broke out. The traditional spiritual leaders of the people blamed the priests for these problems. Intense pressure from all sides forced the local king who had allowed them in to issue an ultimatum: they must leave or they would be driven out. The priests remained. On the day the ultimatum was to take effect, a heavy rainstorm arrived, and the priests were allowed to stay.

Missionaries also ran into problems when international rivalries were carried over into relationships in Angola. In 1884, King Ekwikwi of Bailundo expelled the Congregationalist missionaries from his lands, largely because of information he had received

School Children at the São Salvador Mission, 1907 *This photograph is of the youngest group of students at the São Salvador's elementary school, established by the Reverend Thomas Lewis in 1888 and run by his Baptist mission. Notice the white doll. Also, notice that the child to the right is a mestizo. At first, instruction was in English. However, after a few years, and prodded by Portuguese authorities, Lewis made Portuguese the preferred language. Even Lewis's mission board in London warned him that "missionaries should not seek to make the people Englishmen." By 1893 the Baptist Missionary Society (England) had published a grammar of the Kongo language and had translated the entire New Testament into Kongo. Lewis thought this was most important not only for Christian indoctrination but also for communal identity and self-esteem.*

Just prior to this pioneering missionary school, in 1880, there were only twenty-seven schools in Angola, all supported by the Portuguese government. The statistics do not indicate the racial composition of the 587 students, but since all the schools were in Portuguese administrative centers, we can assume that whether white, mestizo, or black, the pupils were part of the Portuguese community. Of the twenty-seven regular teachers, fourteen were priests and four were women, who taught sixty-two girls in four schools.

from a Portuguese trader named Braga at a time when the Portuguese were very angry with the English. Another missionary, Frederick Arnot, happened to be a guest of the trader Silva Porto at the time, and he went to the king to intervene as soon as he heard what had happened. As a result of their meeting, King Ekwikwi dictated the following letter:

> To Mr. Sanders and Party, Missionaries: I wish you to return with all my heart. I have acted very badly to you and those with you. I have been as one turned, having received you as my friends and children, and then to turn you away as my enemies. Braga persuaded me in a way I could not resist. He told me, in short that to harbor those "English" was to be at war with the Portuguese; that you were people to be killed. . . . The whole country is before you: only return and be friendly with me. I will do my utmost to restore your things. I have eight bales of cloth, also tools, books, etc. belonging to you and your company. All shall be returned. My people are all crying. We are ashamed. Come back! Do not allow our name to stink everywhere because of Braga's deception.

Taylor Faces Criticism

Usually the missionaries avoided such conflicts among themselves, but the case of Bishop Taylor was the exception. Whereas the Roman Catholics were funded by Portugal, and the other Protestants were funded by mission societies, Taylor was determined to make his missions self-supporting. He had already used this approach in India, South Africa, and South America. He believed that external contributions should be used to set up a mission, but that from then on, it should raise its own food and provide for its own needs just as churches in the United States did. He also broke the tradition of sending only religious professionals and possibly medical doctors to other countries. Most of his workers were tradespeople, teachers, and linguists. Because his approach was so different, it invited criticism from traditional missionaries.

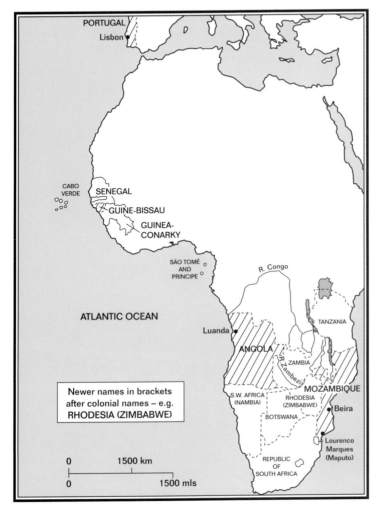

The Portuguese Empire
in Africa

PORTUGAL
Lisbon

CABO
VERDE
SENEGAL
GUINE-BISSAU
GUINEA-
CONARKY

SÃO TOMÉ
AND
PRINCIPE

R. Congo

ATLANTIC OCEAN

TANZANIA

Luanda

ANGOLA

ZAMBIA

MOZAMBIQUE

Newer names in brackets
after colonial names – e.g.
RHODESIA (ZIMBABWE)

S.W. AFRICA
(NAMIBIA)

RHODESIA
(ZIMBABWE)

Beira

BOTSWANA

0   1500 km

0   1500 mls

REPUBLIC
OF
SOUTH AFRICA

Lourenco
Marques
(Maputo)

The Portuguese Empire in Africa

Bishop Taylor planned on establishing his Angolan missions
in the interior, where business was transacted using trade goods
rather than currency. His group had plenty of material for bartering, but very little cash. When it took longer than expected
to move his people inland, they had trouble paying their bills.
Critics described them as ill-prepared and poverty-stricken, not
bothering to explain the extenuating circumstances.

Kongo Member of the Royal Court, c. 1890 *Kongo society was matrilinear—that is, inheritance or descent was determined through the female line. The mother and son in this photograph were of the same royal clan, but the father remained a stranger in the clan sense. By 1920, Portugal had established effective control in all of Angola. That year about 13 percent of the population could trace its ancestry to the Kongo ethnolinguistic group.*

In Angola today there is a nationalist movement led by families who claim that they once belonged to the traditional power structure of the ancient Kongo Kingdom that preceded the Portuguese arrival at the end of the fifteenth century. However, Dom Pedro V (1855–c1895) is considered the last of the reigning Kongo kings. The woman and her son pictured here were members of his royal court. Dom Pedro was placed on the throne by the Portuguese, who maintained a small military garrison in the Kongo capital city of São Salvador to protect him from opposing rival factions. The once mighty Kongo ruler was reduced to a puppet presiding over tribal ceremonies.

The Reverend Thomas Lewis served for almost twenty years as a missionary in Angola for the English Baptist Missionary Society. He arrived in São Salvador in 1887. Shortly after, he was summoned to a "state audience" with Dom Pedro in the "palace," which Lewis described as a mud hut with a grass roof and whitewashed walls. Lewis described what transpired:

> *In honour of our visit, mats, rugs, and leopard-skins covered the walls and floor of the royal apartment, and two chairs were placed for my wife and me to sit on. His Majesty was possessed of a very substantial presence, with a waist of enormous dimensions, and could walk with the utmost difficulty. He had already taken his seat on a gilded throne placed on a raised dais at the end of the room, with a large gilt-framed portrait of "his friend" the King of Portugal, fixed to a wall behind him. His bulky person was encased in a blue and gold military uniform supplied by the [Portuguese] Government, and in his hand he held a silver sceptre; while above all was a cocked hat surmounted with a proud red plume. On that occasion he took a special fancy to a braided dress which my wife wore, and nothing would satisfy him but that he must have a skirt-dress like it made for himself. On remonstrating with him and explaining that only ladies wore that kind of clothing, he immediately replied that is was not so, "for all the Catholic priests wore skirts too!"*

Taylor had arranged for a steamboat to be shipped to Angola in 60-pound packages—the typical weight of materials carried by African porters. When the steamboat arrived in much larger sections, making it impossible to carry above the lower falls to Malebo Pool, other missionaries reported the failure but neglected to mention that the boat had not been shipped as ordered.

In the first four years of the Methodist work in Angola, four members of the group died—not an unusually high number compared to other mission groups. But widely spread false rumors had Bishop Taylor himself dying at sea from disease and all but a couple missionaries dying soon after their arrival.

Critics also complained that the Methodists were spending most of their time simply surviving rather than doing mission work. They seemed to forget that their own leaders were criticized for the same thing by both local Portuguese and the Africans. One Portuguese gunboat commander said of two English missions, "These two missions do everything except mission work; they are tireless travelers, explorers, geographers . . . everything except missionaries." The leader of the Baptists along the Congo River was nicknamed *Vianga-Vianga* (going-going) because of his ceaseless activities.

Other missionary groups were slow to credit the work of Heli Chatelain, the linguist in Taylor's original group. Internationally respected, Chatelain learned Ki-Mbundu (Kimbundu) with the help of Jelemia dia Sabetelu, his Angolan shoemaker. Within two years, Chatelain had published a Kimbundu grammar and translated the Gospel of John into Kimbundu. In 1894, he published *Folk-Tales of Angola: Fifty Tales, with Ki-Mbundu Text, Literal English Translation, Introduction, and Notes.* It remains a significant record of Mbundu culture and tradition. Jelemia's help was so valuable to Chatelain and other linguists that a statue was placed in his honor in the Smithsonian Institution in Washington, D.C.

In general, Protestant missionaries were much more likely to learn the local languages and put them into written form, primarily so that they could translate the Bible into the people's language. This did much to preserve the language and culture of Angola's people. Roman Catholic missionaries focused their energies on teaching Portuguese to Angolans. While all the groups were sincerely committed to improving the lives of Africans, most missionaries could not escape a condescending, paternalistic attitude to those they believed they were "civilizing." And some of them held violently racist views that seriously compromised the Christian message they were trying to communicate.

Bishop Taylor's efforts at establishing self-supporting missions had mixed results. Critics, including some of the original members of the party, maintained that his work was a failure because of the limited numbers of converts made during 11 years of work. Supporters believed that Taylor had succeeded in spreading a general knowledge of Christianity. When the bishop retired in 1896, his unique work in Angola came to an end. The Methodist Missionary Society in America took over all responsibility for the missions and used more traditional methods to support and expand them.

Both Catholic and Protestant missionaries failed to make Christianity a majority religion in Angola during the last quarter of the 1800s. Most Angolans remained loyal to their traditional religious beliefs, including many of those who embraced Christianity. But both groups of missionaries shaped future events in unexpected ways. Through their close association with the Portuguese government, Roman Catholics became partners with them in controlling the lives of Angolans.

Since the Protestants had no stake in Portuguese culture or colonial power, they were often the first foreigners to recognize the injustices faced by both Africans and *mestiços*. This made them effective advocates for reform and unintentional supporters of early Angolan nationalism.

Lunda Fetish Doctors, 1876 *This rare photograph of fetish doctors was taken in the extreme eastern part of Angola near the Congo border. For several centuries the Lunda received Portuguese arms, cloth, and other goods in exchange for ivory and slaves.*

4

THE KINGDOM OF THE KONGO

By the time William Taylor arrived in Angola, the Portuguese had been there for centuries. Their first recorded contact with this part of Africa came in 1483 when Portuguese navigator Diogo Cão reached the mouth of the Congo River. He was met by members of the Kingdom of the Kongo, the most influential power in the region. The Kongo people had migrated to west central Africa over a thousand years before, and their kingdom was more than a century old when Diogo Cão arrived.

At the height of its power, the Kingdom of the Kongo directly controlled an area of 90,000 square miles. From the mouth of the Congo, its territory extended north 100 miles to the Kwilu River and south 200 miles to the Dande, near the modern city of Luanda, Angola. The kingdom stretched inland more than 300 miles, giving it access to Malebo Pool on the Congo. Its eastern boundary included the Kwango River. Because of the sophistication of its trading network and the prestige of its rulers, the economic and political power of the Kingdom of the Kongo reached well beyond these borders, giving it a total sphere of influence covering roughly 200,000 square miles.

Its people were known for their artistic achievements. They mined copper and used it to craft beautiful jewelry, small statues, and religious fetishes. Other mines produced iron ore, which was smelted and then shaped into weapons, tools, ornaments, and even

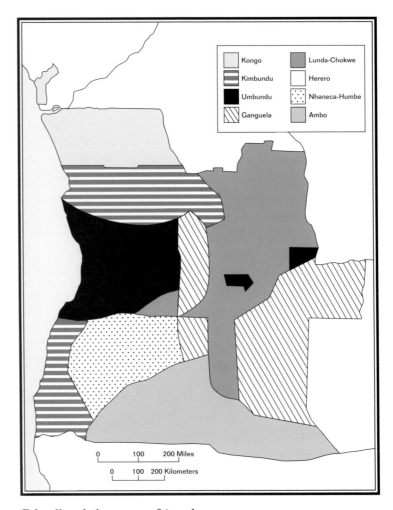

Ethnolinguistic groups of Angola

musical instruments. Because tradition held that the Kingdom of the Kongo had been founded by a blacksmith, the nobility took particular pride in their ironwork.

Their weavers also excelled. Using leaves from the raffia palm tree, along with other vegetable fibers, they created a variety of materials which the Portuguese at first mistook for velvet, damask, brocade, satin, and taffeta. They even made cloth from tree bark.

Other skilled artisans used vines and wicker to create beautiful baskets, nets, and furniture. They carved wood and ivory, and combined the two materials in striking pieces of inlaid furniture. Some of the Kongo people specialized in making pottery.

KONGO GOVERNMENT

Cão was eager to establish diplomatic and trading relations. His first step was to participate in a ritualized exchange of elite hostages. A group of nobles returned with Cão to Portugal and then accompanied him back to the Kongo three years later. Only then was the Portuguese explorer allowed to meet the ManiKongo, who ruled the kingdom.

The government of the ManiKongo included a half-dozen provincial governors appointed by him as well as many less powerful officials, some of whom performed highly specialized duties. For example one person served as *mani vangu vangu,* meaning first judge in cases of adultery. The ManiKongo collected taxes from his people and controlled the currency supply. He settled disputes, dispensed justice, and sought to strengthen his authority by marrying women from influential families.

The ruler of the Kingdom of the Kongo was a revered figure. Anyone who wanted to approach him, had to do so on hands and knees. Anyone who watched him eat or drink was executed. To prevent this from happening, an attendant struck two iron poles together to warn people that their ruler was about to eat. Everyone in sight immediately dropped to the ground and lay face down. Wherever the ManiKongo went he carried a zebra-tail whip as a sign of his authority.

The administrative center of the kingdom was a large town called Mbanza Kongo (The Court of the Kongo), which was located on top of a hill with a commanding view of the surrounding land. Although they didn't write and didn't use the wheel for transportation, the Kongo people had developed systems for measuring distances and time. Travel was described in terms of marching days. It took 10 days to reach Mbanza Kongo from the coast. They used a lunar calendar and had four-day weeks. The first day of each week was a holiday.

Occupational Background of Degredados in Angolia: 1902–14

1) Salaried Workers			2,101
a)	Factory Workers	(707)	
b)	Agricultural Journeymen	(543)	
c)	No Special Designation	(522)	
d)	Domestics	(180)	
e)	Fisherman	(94)	
f)	Clerks	(55)	
2) Self-Employed			347
a)	Farmers	(114)	
b)	Businessmen	(97)	
c)	Property Owners	(68)	
d)	Female Servants	(59)	
e)	Professionals	(6)	
f)	Industrialists	(3)	
3) Military			101
4) No Profession			50
5) Civil Servants			32
6) Beggars			6
7) Prostitute			1
TOTAL			2,638

*Source:*Faria Blanc Junior, O depósito de degredos (Luanda,1916), p. 70-1

They excelled as farmers and grew yams, bananas, and other fruits and vegetables. They raised pigs, goats, and cattle, and fished from area rivers as they still do today. The people also used palm trees for making oil, wine, vinegar, and bread.

As in much of Africa, a limited type of slavery existed. Slaves usually were people who had been captured during a war, had committed some criminal act, or were given by their families as part of a dowry payment. Kongo society was divided into three classes: the nobility, the peasants, and the slaves.

NZINGA MBEMBA

Much of our understanding about Kongo culture comes from Nzinga Mbemba, who is known to history as Affonso I. When the Portuguese first made their way to Mbanza Kongo, Nzinga

Mbemba was a provincial governor. He converted to Christianity, took on the name Affonso, and studied with the priests at the capital for 10 years. He became ManiKongo in 1506 and ruled for almost 40 years. He spoke fluent Portuguese and dictated a long series of letters to Portuguese kings. Dozens of those letters still exist, providing a wealth of information about life in the Kongo before and after the arrival of the Portuguese.

Affonso wanted to modernize his kingdom, using the best of what the Portuguese brought. He supported the Roman Catholic Church and appreciated the value of European medicine. He wanted his people to incorporate the woodworking and masonry techniques used by the Portuguese, and he saw the written word as a valuable commodity. And European weaponry was eagerly used to put down any unrest within his far-flung territory.

But the ManiKongo was careful with the changes he accepted. He refused to adopt the Portuguese legal code and was wary of foreign explorers. He was concerned that rumors about the hidden deposits of gold and silver deep in the interior of his kingdom might turn them from partners to conquerors.

Of all the changes introduced by the Portuguese, Nzinga Mbemba was most disturbed by European slavery. Six years before he took power, a Portuguese expedition had been blown off course and landed in what is now Brazil. Portugal expected great profits from this new land, and within a few decades, a huge demand existed for slaves to run Brazil's mines and coffee plantations. Slaves were also used on Caribbean sugar plantations and eventually were taken to North America.

The existence of African slavery within the Kingdom of the Kongo predisposed chiefs to begin selling slaves to the traders who now descended on Western Africa. But the limited slave trade they had previously known was nothing like the insatiable demands of the Europeans. A trickle of slaves became a flood, and the new wealth from the trade corrupted everyone it touched. Even some priests abandoned their calling and began selling their servants and converts into slavery.

By the 1530s more than 5,000 slaves a year were being shipped across the Atlantic. Many had been purchased more than 700 miles inland and force-marched to the coast. Soon the trails from the interior were littered with the rotting corpses and skeletons of the dead.

The population of Affonso's kingdom began to shrink, and his authority over the village and provincial chiefs disappeared as they grew wealthy from the slave trade. He did not seem to understand that Portugal was more interested in expanding the supply of slaves than in fulfilling its agreements with him for European medicine and technology. In 1526 he wrote a letter to King João III of Portugal:

> The excessive freedom given by your factors and officials to the men and merchants who are allowed to come to this Kingdom . . . is such . . . that many of our vassals, whom we had in obedience, do not comply. We can not reckon how great the damage is, since the above-mentioned merchants daily seize our subjects, sons of the land and sons of our noblemen and vassals and relatives. . . . Thieves and men of evil conscience take them because they wish to possess the things and wares of this Kingdom . . . They grab them and cause them to be sold; and so great, Sir, is their corruption and licentiousness that our country is being utterly depopulated . . . to avoid this, we need from your Kingdoms no other than priests and people to teach in schools, and no other goods but wine and flour for the holy sacrament; that is why we beg your Highness to help and assist us in this matter, commanding the factors that they should send here neither merchants nor wares, because it is our will that in these kingdoms there should not be any trade in slaves nor market for slaves.

This letter, like the many that had preceded it, went unanswered. Finally, in 1529, the king responded: "You . . . tell me that you want no slave-trading in your domains, because this trade is depopulating your country. . . . The Portuguese there, on the contrary, tell me how vast the Congo is, and how it is so thickly populated that it seems as if no slave has ever left."

Affonso sent several letters to the pope, asking him to intervene. But the Portuguese intercepted the messengers who were

Along the shore of the Kunene (Cunene) River, 1923
The Kunene River, which rises in west-central Angola, forms part of the boundary between Angola and Namibia. This common border incorporates a large amount of the traditional winter-grazing lands of the local Vahimba pastoralists. The Vahimba, a Bantu-speaking people, perhaps because of their inaccesible habitat, were the last of the peoples in the area to come under European control.

carrying them as soon as they stepped off the ship in Lisbon. By 1539 complete despair set in when he learned that 10 of his nephews, grandsons, and other relatives whom he had sent to Portugal for a religious education had never arrived. Somewhere during their voyage, the young men had been carried to Brazil, where they became slaves. What could he do when the Portuguese were not even willing to guarantee safe passage for members of his royal family? Nzinga Mbemba died in 1542 or 1543, and his kingdom disintegrated as rival chiefs fought over the riches of the slave trade.

A KINGDOM DISINTEGRATES

In 1568 a further catastrophe engulfed the Kongo people. The Yakas (or Jagas) swept across the kingdom from the southeast frontier near the Kwango River, destroying everything in their path. This warrior nation lived in small, fortified, mobile camps. They killed their own babies to avoid the difficulties of caring for them and raised the older children of their conquered enemies as the next generation of warriors. The Yakas were one of the few African groups to practice cannibalism, and they did it simply to terrify their enemies.

As their enemies advanced, the ManiKongo and his followers fled from the capital. The Yakas plundered and burned the city, feasting on those who had not managed to escape. Then their large force split into many smaller groups and ravaged the rest of the kingdom. Days later, the survivors from the capital took shelter on an island at the mouth of the Congo. Even with Portuguese military help it took two years to drive the invaders out. By then little remained for the ManiKongo to rule. Every village that had survived was in open revolt. Plague and famine further decimated the population. Slave traders and soldiers of fortune roamed at will. By the end of the century, Britain, France, and Holland had joined the slave trade, and even larger numbers of Africans were placed in bondage.

Over the next 250 years, internal conflict and the continuing traffic in slaves further weakened the kingdom. The real power remained in the hands of court officials, provincial governors, and chiefs who ruled over small parts of the kingdom. Together they worked with African merchants to restrict European merchants and explorers to the coastal areas of their realm, but in spite of their efforts, the size of the kingdom continued to shrink.

Occasionally strong monarchs reunited the old kingdom. Henrique II, who reigned from 1845 to 1857, was the last completely independent king of Kongo. His successor, Pedro V (for whom the town of San Pedro was named), gained power with the help of the Portuguese. As the borders between European-controlled areas of Africa were formally established, most

Dom Pedro V Orphanage, Luanda, 1890 *This orphanage was run by the Holy Ghost order in Luanda. Notice the mestizo, or mixed-race, children in the photograph. Throughout the nineteenth century, the Angolan mestizo population was approximately equal to or slightly larger than the white. For example, in 1845 the total Angolan population was estimated at 5.4 million, which included 1,832 (0.03 percent) whites and 5,770 (0.10 percent) mestizos. In that year, there were almost 11 white men for every white woman in Angola. This ratio changed slightly by 1900. The total population then stood at about 4.8 million—9,198 (0.20 percent) whites and 3,112 (0.06 percent) mestizos.*

Mestizos held key posts in business, the civil service, journalism, the military, and politics. They seldom, if ever, identified with the Africans, because for all practical purposes they were Portuguese in every way but color. Between 1912 and 1925 at least two mestizos were mayors of Luanda. As the white population increased, the outnumbered mestizos lost their privileged position. Nevertheless, the mestizos continued to identify with the Portuguese in the struggles between Europeans and Africans. Even though they were second-class citizens, they ranked above the blacks, who were not regarded as citizens but as "natives."

House in the São Salvador Mission Compound, 1907 *Note the tripod to the left of this house in the mission established by the Reverend Thomas Lewis. It was probably used for a surveying instrument.*

Lewis wrote that São Salvador was no different from any other town in the Kongo province. June to August were rainless and the heat unrelenting. The rocky soil reflected the sun's rays, making them often unbearable. November through May were the rainy months. But the surrounding valley seemed fertile and well-cultivated despite the hoe being the only implement used. The principal crops were manioc, yams, corn, various types of beans, and pumpkins. Pumpkin seeds were considered a delicacy. Meat consumption consisted of domestic fowl and goat. Pigs were kept as pets and pork rarely eaten. The many swamps contained eel and catfish, which were caught by means of small bottle-shaped basket traps made of split bamboo. The fish were arranged on a spit about a yard long, then preserved by being smoked over a fire.

of the Kingdom of the Kongo came under the personal control of Leopold II, king of the Belgians, as part of the Congo Free State. The former capital of the once-great realm remained a part of Portuguese Angola. Although most Portuguese had long known it as São Salvador, the Kongo people still remembered its true name—Mbanza Kongo. And through all the centuries of change, they refused to forget its proud history.

Crossing the Kwanza (Cuanza) River, 1920

The Kwanza River drains most of the central Angola and it is the only Angolan river of any economic significance.

5

THE MBUNDU

Opportunity. That's what Ndambi aNgola, king of the Ndongo, saw in the late 1560s as he gathered reports about the Yakas' (or Jagas') attacks on the Kingdom of the Kongo and the Portuguese. His land belonged to the Kingdom of the Kongo, but with the ManiKongo's power weakening, he had the perfect opportunity to assert his people's independence.

The Ndongo were part of the larger Mbundu group located south and east of the Kingdom of the Kongo. A well-established society based on agriculture, the Mbundu were also known for their metal-working. The Ndongo called their king the *ngola* after a sacred relic made from a small piece of metal that symbolized authority within a family line. Just as the Portuguese got the name for the Kongo from the title of its ruler, the ManiKongo, so they began to call the area around the Kwanza River valley "Angola" after the title of its leader, the ngola.

Ndambi aNgola had many reasons for wanting independence from the ManiKongo. His wealth and power would increase dramatically once he stopped paying tribute to another king. As the independent ruler of the Mbundu people, he would be free to find new ways to protect them from the slave traders who were appearing more frequently in his territory. He wanted to create a new facility for the export of slaves that could compete with Mpinda, at the mouth of the Congo River. Some of the Portuguese traders already supported this idea because it would allow them to avoid the taxes charged at the official port and thus increase their profits. As a partner of the slave traders, Ndambi aNgola hoped to influence them to look for captives beyond the borders of the Mbundu kingdom. What he didn't realize was that Portugal would not be satisfied with simply gathering the profits from the quickly expanding slave trade. The first Portuguese governor to Ngondo was a young noble-man named Paul Dias de Novães. He schemed to create a trade monopoly with Ngondo because he believed huge silver mines lay in the interior. Dias agreed to colonize Angola for Portugal at his own expense in return for getting the southern part of the area as his own private property. Ndambi aNgola and the rest of the Ndongo knew nothing of these plans.

PORTUGUESE EXPANSION

At first Dias stayed with about 400 men on the island of Luanda. In 1575 the ngola died. His successor was caught up fighting rebels who questioned his authority. Dias quietly moved to the mainland where he built the coastal city of Luanda, but he kept his eye on the civil war. He did not want it to cause problems for Portuguese traders. By 1579 Dias was ready to stake a claim on the rumored silver mines. He marched with troops up the Kwanza River valley, a move that was inter-preted by the ngola as an act of war.

For the next 40 years, the Portuguese and Ngondo fought with each other as the Portuguese attempted again and again to head inland. Not only were they looking for silver mines, which they never found, but they were also searching for a water passage to the Indian Ocean. Ignorant of the interior geography of central Africa, they believed traders' reports that only 100 to 300 miles separated Ngondo from the eastern coast of Africa. If they could somehow connect from the Kwanza River to the Indian Ocean, they would significantly reduce the length, expense, and risk of potentially lucrative voyages to India and the Far East.

While the Europeans had superior fire power, they were far more susceptible to tropical diseases and parasitic infections.

By 1592, 1,700 Portuguese men had been lost either to illness, battle casualties, or desertion. Only 300 Portuguese remained in Angola, and they had to rely on help from Africans who they feared might turn on them at any moment. A continuing line of ngolas, meanwhile, made concerted efforts to confine the Portuguese to the coast. Each side savored tremendous victories; each side also suffered huge defeats.

Nzinga's Journey to Power

In 1622 a Ngondo woman appeared on the scene who would become a larger-than-life character and is still held up as a heroine by many Angolans. Nzinga was a half-sister to the reigning ngola. She took an impressive party of court officials and servants to Luanda, where she oversaw negotiations with the Portuguese. Because it was a necessary part of the peace process, she was baptized and took on the name Ana da Sousa. A treaty duly agreed to, she returned to her brother. In less than a year, the ngola mysteriously died, and Nzinga remains the primary suspect in his death, in part because she immediately claimed the throne.

The Ngondo traditionally did not accept women rulers, and Nzinga did not possess the correct ancestry for the role in any event. She spent the next 40 years—the rest of her life—manipulating African and European neighbors to make sure that she retained her power. At one point, she joined forces with the Jagas. She also welcomed escaped slaves from Portuguese-controlled territory and convinced African soldiers to desert the Portuguese and join her by promising them land and other riches. When the Portuguese took steps to replace her as ruler of the Ngondo and forced her from the land, she moved further east, to the Mbundu state of Matamba, which had a tradition of women as rulers. Because she was an enemy of the Portuguese, she was very popular with other Africans. She overthrew Matamba's sitting queen with the help of the Jaga and became Matamba's next ruler. Allying herself with the Dutch, during the 1640s she built Matamba into a significant force in the region and saw the Dutch drive the Portuguese from Luanda. When the Portuguese again possessed Luanda, Nzinga made peace with them and ruled over Matamba and much of what was Ngondo until her death in 1663.

Mestizo Boy, Luanda, 1876

COLONIZATION

Nzinga's stand against the Portuguese became legendary among Africans as the Portuguese increased their influence over the Mbundu people. By 1700 Angola was considered the first significant Portuguese colony in Africa. It possessed a governing structure that remained largely in place for the next 200 years. Angola was divided into **presidios,** each headed by a military commander who acted as absolute ruler. A *presidio* was divided into chiefdoms ruled by African chiefs who paid tributes to the military commander, much as they had previously done to their kings. The significant changes were that the fees were much greater than they had been in the past and that rule was by force, with little thought given to justice. Commenting on the military commanders, historian Jan Vansima observed, "The cardinal principal of their policy was to take as much as possible from their subjects, and still avoid a general rebellion. Indeed, whenever Portuguese arms were unsuccessful, such a rebellion followed almost automatically in most *presidios.*" Because the forces that were stationed with the military commanders were small, the risk for such uprisings was great.

Luanda was ruled by a town council called the **camara,** which advised the governor-general of the colony and took over the government in his absence. Other important officials included the chief justice and the commander of the army. Portugal did not pay salaries for any of these positions. Instead, the officials depended on the slave trade and on siphoning off government income. This meant that the *camara* constantly pushed for wars within Angola to increase the supply of slaves, and therefore the money they could get from the slave trade. The governor-general regularly exacted fees from Africans whom he appointed to various jobs. The chief justice kept part of the fines, compromising his desire to exact true justice, and the military kept a fixed percentage of the spoils from war, including slaves. The entire system was designed to oppress the Africans and expand the slave trade.

On rare occasions, a new governor would try to reform the system, but if he didn't quickly conform to the existing structure, he was sent packing by mobs or the military. Most governors didn't attempt to institute change. They simply got through their short assignment to Luanda by making as much money as possible.

Because of the expense of wars in Europe and instability in the Portuguese government, Portugal was never able to invest the military forces or money needed to completely occupy the Mbundu lands. What efforts they made were further hindered by continuing struggles with disease. *Presidios* were sometimes deserted because the local army commander could not suppress African revolts. In spite of these problems, the basic colonial government remained the same, and some Africans and *mestiços,* people of both Portuguese and African ancestry, helped the Portuguese increase their influence throughout the area.

This was particularly true at Mbaka, a Portuguese settlement about 170 miles east of Luanda. An important trading center, it was populated by many African-Portuguese who specialized in supplying slaves and ivory for the coastal merchants. (There were few Portuguese women in Luanda, much less in the interior, so Portuguese men often married African women.) These people became known as Ambakistas after the name of their settlement. They spoke both Kimbundu, the language of the Mbundu peoples, and Portuguese, and in some cases could write in Portuguese as well. They made use of both their ties to the Portuguese and their ties to local African families to further their trade. They had fewer problems with disease than did their Portuguese counterparts on the coast, who were happy to leave the dangers of inland trade to the Ambakistas.

The Ambakistas proudly served in the Portuguese army, helping to put down rebellions among oppressed African communities. They were credited or blamed by both Europeans and Africans for doing more than any other group to open the Kwanga, Kuilu, and Kassai River basins to the Portuguese. So closely were they associated with the colonial power, that the Swiss-American missionary and linguist Heli Chatelain noted in

Ambro People, 1890 *The Ambro people straddled the border between Angola and Namibia. In Angola they made up less than 3 percent of the population in 1920, yet they owned most of Angola's cattle and were the principal suppliers of beef steer and of young animals for the central highlands. The possession of cattle gave these people a special status.*

There were some twenty-odd clans among the Ambro. Each clan had its own king. The last king with any real authority was defeated by the Portuguese in 1915. The Ambro capital, Onjiva, near the border with Namibia, was given the name of the conquering general, Pereira d'Eca. These proud people, when pressed by Portuguese colonialism, were able to cross the Namibian border to maintain their lifestyle. At the time of Angola's independence (1975), the capital, Pereira d'Eca, was renamed Onjiva.

his 1894 book, *Folk-Tales of Angola,* that the Ki-Mbundu term *mundele,* meaning "white person," was used to refer to them.

The Mbundu peoples experienced Portuguese exploitation longer than any other groups in Angola. They were sold into slavery, and when slavery became illegal, they were forced to work under equally oppressive circumstances. Their lands were seized and turned into coffee plantations, which their labor supported.

BEGINNINGS OF PROTEST

As the end of the 1800s approached, the Mbundu became the first group in Angola to experience "effective occupation" by the Portuguese. Yet the beginnings of protest arose among the Mbundu as well. Encouraged by Heli Chatelain, educated Mbundu began writing down their oral traditions and developing their own literature. Between 1870 and 1926, the press in

Luanda Coaling Company, Luanda, 1899
The Portugese depended upon coal as the energy source to run their railroads. Since Angola produced virtually no coal, it was necessary to import it from the southeastern Congo (Kinshasa).

Main Street, Luanda, 1899 *Luanda is the capital of Angola and the country's largest city. It was founded in 1576 and is the oldest Portuguese settlement south of the equator. It was the center for exporting slaves. In 1900, the city had a total population of about 25,000.*

Between the late sixteenth century and 1836, when Portugal abolished the "legal" slave trade, it is estimated that Angola provided more than 2 million slaves for the New World. More than half went to Brazil; a third to the Caribbean and about 10 to 15 percent to the Río de la Plata area on the southeastern coast of South America. Most of these slaves passed through the port of Luanda.

Besides exporting slaves, the merchants of Luanda kept slaves as porters, soldiers, agricultural laborers, and as workers at jobs that the Portuguese increasingly considered too menial to do themselves. However, at no time was domestic slavery more important to the local economy than the exporting of slaves.

Portugese Naval Station on Island Facing Luanda, C. 1940
This naval station became extremely important between 1961–65 when Portugal increased its armed forces in Angola from 9,000 to 50,000 officers and men.

The São Salvador Infirmary, 1907 *Mrs. Lewis, the wife of the Reverend Thomas Lewis, who established this infirmary, served as the doctor, nurse, and midwife. She is standing in the doorway next to her aide.*

Angola and Portugal was relatively free, a situation utilized by educated *mestiços*. On April 8, 1882, José de Fontes Pereira made the following statement in a weekly Portuguese newspaper published in Luanda:

> How has Angola benefited under Portuguese rule? The darkest slavery, scorn and the most complete ignorance! And even the government have done their utmost to the extent of humiliating and vilifying the sons of this land who do possess the necessary qualifications for advancement. . . . What a civiliser, and how Portuguese!

A lawyer born in Luanda, this educated *mestiço* was one of a small number of voices openly questioning why Portugal should continue to have a role in governing Angola. From this small start, a significant nationalist movement was to be born.

Mestizo, 1890 *Between 1777 and 1960, the mestizo population of Angola never exceeded 01.10 percent of the total. In the 1960s after a number of generations, the ancestors of many mestizo became so mixed that the Portuguese mandated a set of distinctions among them. Many mestizos accepted this system as a means of social ranking. For example, the term* mestizo *used alone applied specifically to the offspring of a mulatto and a white; the term* mestizo cabrito *referred to the descendant of a union between two mulattos; and the term* mestizo cafuso *was applied to the child of a union between a mulatto and a black African.*

Most mestizos were urban dwellers and had learned to speak Portuguese either as a household language or at school. Almost all mestizo identified with Portuguese culture.

6

THE OVIMBUNDU

As it usually does, the bad news spread quickly from person to person. Initial reactions of disbelief gradually shifted to horrified acceptance. The kings had been taken by their enemies. No one knew when or if they would return.

To the Bailundo and Ndulu kingdoms, it was almost too much to bear. Members of the Ovimbundu people, they prided themselves in their warriors' capabilities. Yet in spite of their stone fortifications built from stone formations that were the gifts of the gods and their rulers, in spite of their elevated position on the highlands, some 5,000 feet above sea level, they had lost. Lost badly.

It was no consolation to them that their fortification has been too strong to be taken outright. The lengthy siege waged by the Portuguese and their African allies had worn the Ovimbundu down. Finally, under cover of darkness, they had fled to relative safety. It took almost two months for the Portuguese and their allies to tear down their stone walls, but ultimately the walls came down. The area was sacked. Humiliating as it was, this story would be passed down from generation to generation. It was necessary. How else would their children's children understand why a proud warrior race had turned to trade as their primary activity? How else could they explain that sometimes ultimate victory rose up from the worst defeats?

ORIGINS OF THE OVIMBUNDU

The Ovimbundu had probably existed as a group of roughly 22 cooperative kingdoms for less than 100 years when the Portugese so convincingly defeated the Bailundu and Ndulu in a series of battles between 1774 and 1776. They began to be identified as a unique group when the feared Jagas had invaded from the northeast, taken over, and shaped their societies. Living in the Benguela Highlands, on top of a roughly 5,000-foot high escarpment, they were largely protected from surprise attacks. While slight differences in language existed from one kingdom to the next, they all spoke variations of Umbundu and were able to understand each other easily.

In many ways, life was comfortable. Although they lived in the tropics, their high elevation moderated their weather patterns and temperatures. The highs rarely went over 90 degrees in the summer, and the lows in the winter usually didn't drop below freezing. The area was quite beautiful, a fact not lost on Commander V. L. Cameron during his travels from Zanzibar to Benguela in 1875:

> As we went forward the scenery increased in beauty, and at last I was constrained to halt and surrender myself to the enjoyment of the view which lay before me.

> I will content myself with asserting that nothing could be more lovely than this entrancing scene, this glimpse of Paradise. To describe it would be impossible....

> In the foreground were glades in the woodland, varied with knolls crowned by groves of large, English-looking trees, sheltering villages with yellow thatched roofs; . . . plantations with the fresh green of young crops and the bright red of newly hoed ground in vivid contrast, and running streams flashing in the sunlight; while in the far distance were mountains of endless and pleasing variety of form, gradually fading away until they blended with the blue of the sky. . . .

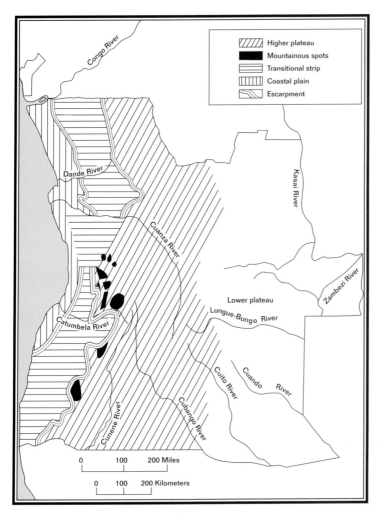

Topography and rivers of Angola.

That evening we camped in a wood, a clear space having literally to be cut out of the masses of sweet-scented creepers which festooned the trees.

Women raised primarily maize and beans for food, and other needs were provided by the men either trading with or raiding their neighbors. Cattle, for instance, came from herds raised by

Vahimba, c. 1920 *These Vahimba are making fire by striking flint to cause a spark. The Vahimba live along the banks of the Kunene River in west-central Angola.*

people to the south. They also took slaves as part of the spoils of their frequent wars and used them in their villages or traded them for supplies. Large iron deposits supported a metal-crafts industry that also contributed to trade.

The people of the Benguela Highlands had known of the Portuguese presence in Africa since at least the 1500s. The Ovimbundu had on occasion allied themselves with the Portuguese against other African groups, and sometimes they joined forces with the Dutch against the Portuguese. Through trade, they had acquired trade cloth, from which they made their clothes, as well as guns. But the Portuguese had not attempted to penetrate the Benguela Highlands, because from the coast it was easier to move into the Congo River and Kwanza River valleys. To reach the Ovimbundu, the Portuguese had to cross an arid region that lay between the coast and the highlands.

Apparently the event that triggered the Portuguese attack on the Ovimbundu in 1774 was that the Ovimbundu were trading with the French. This concerned the Portuguese for two reasons: they wanted the area to be closed to trade with any European power other than themselves, and they disliked the French because 12 years earlier, during the Seven Years' War, France had joined with Spain and invaded Portugal.

Sᴜʀᴠɪᴠᴀʟ Tʜʀᴏᴜɢʜ Tʀᴀᴅᴇ

Driven from their own fortifications, the Ovimbundu decided to build a mutually beneficial trade relationship with Portugal. Rather than raid Portuguese *presidios* or steal from Portuguese traders, they became the major supplier of slaves to the port cities of Luanda and Benguela. As demand grew, the Ovimbundu traveled further into the interior, and assisted Portuguese traders and explorers such as Silva Porto and Serpa Pinto. On occasion they reached the east coast of Africa, and they discouraged eastern traders from venturing into Ovimbundu territory by lying about conditions. The independent kingdoms within the Ovimbundu, however, reached informal agreements that allowed each others caravans to travel unimpeded through their territory. Over the next 100 years, the Ovimbundu took hundreds of thousands of Africans to slave ships on the coast, where their captives were transported mostly to Brazil and the Caribbean Islands. (Slaves going to North America usually traveled on ships belonging to British and U.S. merchants.) Some trade was done in other areas, such as ivory and beeswax, but 80 percent of the value of all exports from the Portuguese colony was slaves.

The result of all this activity was that in general the Ovimbundu became rather wealthy. Women and girls provided food for the caravans that would usually be gone for months at a

time. Boys traveled with the men from the time they were about 10 years old, learning the ins and outs of bartering, negotiating, and other skills needed to be a successful trader. The fact that they were building their business on the backs of human suffering was not an issue to them. The slave trade was an expansion of their traditional activities, and the Jaga had been a major force in the slave trade before they took over the Ovimbundu.

When the slave trade became illegal in 1836, demand did not decrease. Aside from trade cloth, the Ovimbundu accepted large amounts of rum from Brazil in exchange for the slaves they brought to the coast. So while the Ovimbundu were disrupting the lives of interior groups with the slave trade, their own lives were being disrupted by alcohol abuse. According to Ngalangi tradition, so much rum was present in the Ovimbundu kingdoms from the time of King Ndumba II (about 1840) on that it was poured into troughs and drunk by men, women, and children.

Slave trade continued through the rest of the century, but in 1874 a shift in trade began. That is when caravans going into the interior began carrying out what was called first-class rubber. This rubber was harvested from the vines of wild rubber plants, which grew up the huge trees of the rainforest. Initially the distance and time involved in harvesting the plant kept it

Hunting Guides, c. 1928 *Hunting guides assisted numerous European big-game hunters who came to Angola in the 1920s. The prized animal was the Giant Sable, an antelope with the longest horns of any game animal. Today this animal is almost extinct.*

By the mid-1920s, the Portuguese had completed a grid of roads linking major Angolan economic centers. For example, one road ran from Luanda into the Congo to the north, another to Namibia in the south, and a major road almost reached the Zambian border. One hunter reported in 1928 that "motor services" along these roads had become increasingly popular—"the cars are usually loaded to their fullest capacity . . . and one can stop to shoot a buck or a bird." But these roads remained unpaved. Even by 1953, Angola had only fifty-three miles of asphalted roads.

from being significantly more profitable than beeswax, so until 1886 it was simply one of many items the Ovimbundu brought out to the coast.

A major breakthrough came in 1886 when an Ovimbundu caravan brought a load of "red rubber" from the sandy country east of the Kwanza River. While it took at least eight months to bring out loads of first-class rubber, only three months was needed to transport the red rubber. At first the red rubber got lower prices, but when people discovered that it had unique qualities that made it superior, the price shot up. The Ovimbundu began concentrating their efforts on bringing out red rubber. In 1891 the amount of red rubber exported from Benguela was 16 times greater than it had been just five years before, and it was worth three and one-half times the value of the three leading exports combined in 1886.

With such lucrative business at hand, anyone who was able to carry a load joined the caravans. Suddenly girls were expected to travel with the trading parties as well. Only the women and the infirm stayed at home to raise the crops which provided rations necessary for the caravans when they were traveling through areas where they could not trade for food. Working on the caravans was more profitable than working for the Europeans, so the Portuguese and other foreigners had difficulty finding porters to work for them. Mission schools suffered from sparse attendance because parents were reluctant to allow children to stay home and go to school when they could be making money in the rubber trade.

THE LAST GREAT RULER

One of the best-known and most admired Ovimbundu kings of this period was Ekwikwi II of Bailundu. He came to the stool, as Ovimbundu thrones were called, in 1876, just as the rubber trade was beginning to enter Ovimbundu life. As that trade became more important, Ekwikwi oversaw the growth of agriculture in his kingdom. Because caravans were spending more time away from their home villages, they needed more food for the road. That fact, along with a growing market of food products at the coast, transformed Ovimbundu agriculture

Angolan Village, 1876

from a small activity intended to provide for seasonal needs to a large activity designed to supply more than the people in the immediate communities.

Ekwikwi also adapted the traditional role of warfare during his reign. Rather than launching large-scale operations that would provoke Europeans and powerful Ovimbundu neighbors, he confined himself to smaller skirmishes. He also recognized the need of securing his own position in the kingdom because the increasing riches of all Ovimbundu gave power to people who in the past would have stayed on the lower rungs of society. Family lineage no longer carried the singular prestige it once had.

Angolans photographed at a Protestant Mission, c. 1925

The Portugese authorities, especially after 1950, considered the influence of the Protestant missions to be that of foreign agents who exerted a subversive influence over the native population.

A 1960's Portugese secret government document noted that the Protestant missionaries generated "admiration and enthusiasm for certain anti-Portugese ideologies and movements. They surreptitiously undermine the idea of Portugese citizenship. They create mentalities in the service of ideas inimical to Portugal. At best, they limit themselves to propagating a religious ideology not in conformity with our tradition. They neutralize our efforts for Portugalization and occupy key positions which make it easy for them to implant ideas contrary to our interests."

Ekwikwi had only to look at his neighbor to the southeast, the kingdom of Viye, to be warned of the dangers inherent in his changing world. After a series of coups that overthrew the traditional head of the kingdom, Ndunduma came to power in 1888. His refusal to take the advice of Silva Porto combined with the high-handedness of the Portuguese captain Paiva Couceiro led to a disastrous war with the Portuguese. The Viye dependence on magical protection against bullets failed, Ndunduma was exiled to the Cape Verde Islands, and the once-proud Viye Kingdom came under the rule of a king chosen by the Portuguese and overseen by troops at a local fort.

Portugal had begun a concerted effort to achieve effective occupation of the Benguela Highlands. By the close of 1892, 135 Portuguese soldiers were stationed in Viye. In Bailundu, Ekwikwi himself had to tolerate the presence of two African soldiers who were in the pay of the Portuguese. Tradition says they smuggled themselves in disguised as porters carrying trade goods.

This relatively minor representation of Portuguese authority would not last for long. The next year, Ekwikwi died, and by 1896 the battle with the Portuguese over control of Bailundu had begun. The days of self-governing rule and local control of trade were numbered.

Two Carriers, 1923 *In 1923 Colonel John C. B. Statham and his wife embarked on a 1,000-mile expedition through southern Angola, across the Kalahari Desert of northern Botswana, ending at the Victoria Falls in northwestern Zimbawe. The colonel had a great deal of difficulty with these two Angolan carriers. In fact, obtaining local assistance was a constant problem for him throughout the Angolan part of his expedition. The colonel found fault with the two carriers in this photograph "for only taking our loads, weighing 50 lbs each, but 9 miles [in one day]." "They kept complaining," he wrote, "of their inability to march without food, though they found a great abundance of 'Mabola' plums and other forest foods on which they had been living for many weeks past." On previous expeditions, Statham, a wealthy English landowner, had been mauled by a bear in India and trampled on by a rhinoceros in East Africa.*

During his Angolan expedition, he and his wife traveled by boats of various kinds, oxen-drawn wagons, canoes, porter-carried hammocks, and on foot. They followed the Okavango River system from central Angola (where it is known as the Kubango) to Botswana's Kalahari Desert—and British protection. From there to the Victoria Falls the route was well charted.

The couple returned to England in October 1923, and the following year, the colonel wrote With My Wife Across Africa by Canoe and Caravan *(1924). He dedicated the book to his wife for her courage.*

7

THE BAILUNDU REVOLT

It began in a seemingly innocent way. Early in 1902 Ovimbundu gathered to celebrate the inauguration of Kalandula as paramount chief of Bailundu, one of their major kingdoms. The event became a huge party, featuring drumming, dancing, and beer-drinking. Portuguese traders in the area saw the inauguration as an opportunity to make money, and lots of it. They inflated prices. One trader sold five kegs of rum for five slaves. Another trader sold two kegs of rum to an Ovimbundu chief, Mutu ya Kevela, but the chief, in accordance with Ovimbundu trading custom, said that he would pay later once he had returned from a rubber-collecting trip. In an act calculated to shame Mutu ya Kevela, the trader insisted on payment while the celebration was still going on. This offended not only Mutu ya Kevela, but also his fellow rulers.

The trader left but returned later, threatening to take Mutu ya Kevela as a slave if he did not pay immediately. As word of this insult spread throughout Bailundu, simmering anger reached a boil. The American missionary Robert G. Moffat reported to his board, "This was more than the Chief and the old men could stand, to see one of them taken as a slave."

When Mutu ya Kevela refused once again to pay up, the Portuguese trader decided to appeal to a higher authority. He went to the nearby Bailundu fort and lodged a formal report of the matter to the captain major, who in turn summoned Mutu ya Kevela and gave him 10 days to pay or else face more fines. Legally, the captain major could not impose fines, but it was common practice for these Portuguese officials to take such action anyway.

Tensions mounted. With the support of other Ovimbundu leaders, Mutu ya Kevela stood firm. The captain major sent a sergeant and two soldiers to demand payment. They were greeted with insults and mocking from the Ovimbundu and returned to the fort empty-handed. They reported that Mutu ya Kevela would not recognize the captain major's authority over him.

Neither side felt they could back down. The Bailundu leaders began meeting regularly, and unknown people spread the word, "Shoot . . . Drive out all Portuguese; we are tired of trouble and rum." Soon hundreds of people gathered on a hill that overlooked the Portuguese fort. They jeered and shouted insults. Rumors of war circulated widely. Terrified white traders sought refuge at the fort. Within days, violence would rip apart the area and change life in Bailundu forever.

SEEDS OF REVOLT

As in most major conflicts, the incident that seemed to provoke the violence was actually a flashpoint. The real problems had been building for years. The Bailundu and their other Ovimbundu neighbors had never been happy with the Portuguese presence as represented by three local forts scattered throughout the Benguela Highlands. They were staffed by small, ill-trained, poorly equipped, and ineffective personnel. Many of the soldiers were *degradados,* people convicted of crimes such as homicide and theft in Portugal and sent to Angola as part of their punishment.

But of greater concern to the Ovimbundu were the Portuguese traders in the area. Ever since 1890, when Silva Porto had committed suicide and the Portuguese had established a military presence in the region, the number of white traders in the interior of Benguela had grown until it reached about 1,600. Most of these traders were agents for coastal trading companies and were also *degradados.*

Although previously the Ovimbundu had enjoyed mutually beneficial trading relationships with Portuguese traders, now they themselves were being harassed. Armed white traders attacked their caravans, captured their people, and sold them into forced labor. Appealing to the captain major did no good. He always backed the *degradados* and often would impose punishments on the Africans.

Forced Labor

Even though Portugal had made slavery illegal in 1878, the practice continued under the concept called "forced labor." Throughout the colony of Angola, any African man who was deemed to be a "vagrant," usually defined as not working for a European or his African agent, could be forced to work anywhere in the colony. Often these men were marched hundreds of miles to the coast, where they would work on coffee, sugar, or cocoa plantations. Thousands were shipped from the ports of Luanda and Benguela to the Portuguese islands of São Tomé and Principe, located off the coast of west Africa.

Workers were supposed to receive five-year contracts, but usually those contracts were never explained to the Africans or even given to them. A person who held someone's contract could sell it—and the worker—to a third party, creating a legal slave trade. When the five years were up, workers were rarely dismissed from their jobs. These ***serviçais,*** as the contract employees were called, were given just enough food, clothing, and shelter to survive. Some critics claimed that they were treated worse than slaves had been in the past. Many *serviçais* did not survive the first five years of their work. Seldom did families see their loved ones again after they had been forced into service.

Missionary accounts of atrocities were dismissed by Portuguese officials, but even some Portuguese recorded what was happening to the Africans. Belo de Almeida, a Portuguese soldier in Angola at the time, gave this account:

It was the custom in those days to give them [*serviçais*] the rudest and most difficult work, in domestic service as well as in the fields and factories, above all in the matter of porterage, in which they took the role of humble animals.

For the slightest fault they were often cruelly punished by being beaten with the hippopotamus-hide whip which cut their skin horribly. Very frequently one heard in the late hour of a warm mysterious African night piercing shrieks of pain from the poor wretches who were being beaten by the company officers or head men, generally hard-hearted mulattoes.

Underlying the concept of forced labor was a racist attitude toward African people in general. Ferreira do Amaral, the Portuguese delegate to the Sixth International Geographical Conference held in London in 1895, gave this explanation of African labor:

We hear people today talk about imported or forced labor and we equally hear the *gros mot* of "slavery" which has been used so often to exploit the tender-hearted people of Europe. For me, the [African] will never work willingly, and the only way to oblige him to work is to make him pay dearly for the satisfaction of his few necessities. This has been the economic policy of Portugal in Africa.

The cruelty and disruption to daily life brought by forced labor filled Africans with fear. Villages were moved from the main trade routes into the thicker forest in a vain attempt to escape the notice of white traders who were hunting for people to make *serviçais*. Women and children were not immune, although legally they were not supposed to be included. Children carrying heavy loads for white masters continued to be a common sight.

As the rubber trade continued to grow, the search for workers intensified. Whole villages would be commandeered into marching hundreds of miles to extract latex from rubber plants and then carry the precious material back to the coast. If the men of a village had already been pressed into service in another part of the colony, the women and children were forced to harvest the rubber.

The government did nothing to investigate who was doing the work and under what conditions. Working for a government that was experiencing financial problems, Angola's officials were satisfied to continue collecting export duties on rubber. They understood that Portugal wanted two things from its colony: money to fill the treasury, and effective occupation of the land to prevent any further blows to Portuguese pride. The government was extremely aware of continuing threats from Britain to occupy parts of Angola and Mozambique. One Portuguese government had already been overthrown because of what the Portuguese people perceived as giving up Portuguese land in Africa to Britain. The new government had no desire to repeat such a mistake.

Another policy that fed the anger in the Benguela Highlands and in other regions of Angola was the seizing of land. If an area was perceived as not being claimed, and the Africans had no say in how such judgments were made, Portuguese residents could seize the land for themselves. Thousands of acres of African land were converted into coffee, sugar, and cotton plantations, and local Africans were pressed into labor on these new Portuguese holdings.

THE BAILUNDU REVOLT

Finally, the Ovimbundu were tired of the Portuguese interfering in their internal government. Beginning with the replacement of Ndunduma, the local captain major had become accustomed to selecting rulers for area kingdoms when he did not approve of the people's choice. When the captain major insisted that Mutu ya Kevela pay the trader or face additional fines, the Ovimbundu leaders determined that they had taken their last insult and were no longer going to allow this Portuguese officer to take advantage of them. They laid siege to the fort. In late April, Paramout Chief Kalandula entered the fort, ostensibly to make peace. In reality he was buying time for the other leaders to organize a revolt throughout the area. This revolt

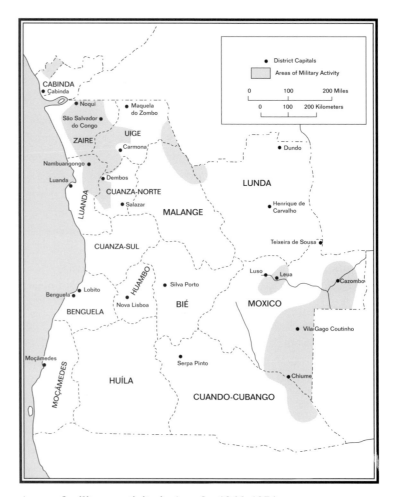

Areas of military activity in Angola, 1966–1974.

broke out earlier than planned, and the Portuguese seized Kalandula as a prisoner. The captain major managed to get a message
out to the coast, but he misrepresented what was happening.

Portuguese authorities sent in three armed columns to assault
the three major kingdoms of the Benguela Highlands. Although
they had superior arms, they were slowed by illness and by an
impressive offensive from the Ovimbundu. Using outdated
muzzle-loaders and lacking lead for cartridges, the men stuffed
their guns with nails and crushed stones. They cut off commu-

nication lines between the Portuguese and their support base at the coast. A surprised governor-general later said, "All . . . seemed to have been engineered by a very well experienced general [rather] than by a savage. . . . The importance of the communication service which some people don't pay more attention to is clearly understood by these savages."

It took four months, but by the middle of September, the Bailundu Revolt, as it came to be called, was over. Ultimately the superior arms of the Portuguese and their African allies made the difference. The Benguela Highlands were under the firm control of the Portuguese. Mutu ya Kevela, whose stand against the Portuguese trader and captain major had helped trigger the events, was killed in battle. But a government review of the events was about to bring major changes to how business was conducted in the interior of Angola.

Kasanje Chief, 1906 *Kasanje was a historic African kingdom on the upper Kwango River in what is now Angola. It was founded about 1620 by a group from Lunda led by a warrier named Kasanje. (Lunda is an area of Bantu-speaking people scattered over wide areas of eastern Angola, the southeastern part of Congo, and northen and north-western Zambia.) The Kasanje conquered and settled the plains west of the Kwango and named the new state after their leader.*

By the mid-seventeeth century, Kasanje enjoyed a thriving trade with Lunda and other states of the African interior. It also established commercial ties with Portuguese traders on the Atlantic coast. At the market of Cassange, the capital of Kasanje, Por-tuguese merchants bartered for slaves. Kasanje repulsed several Portuguese military expeditions in the mid-nineteenth century. However, in 1910–1911, most of Kasanje was incorporated into Portuguese Angola.

8

CONQUEST

With the Bailundu Revolt subdued, peace talks began at the end of September 1902. They included an investigation into why the revolt had happened in the first place. Among the participants was Wesley Stover, an American Congregationalist missionary. As far as is known, Stover did not file a report of the hearings, and the official Portuguese report does not include a record of what the Ovimbundu related. One thing is clear: for once, at least some of the Portuguese offenders were held responsible for their actions.

A majority of the Portuguese traders in the area were found guilty of abuses and exiled. The captains major of two of the three forts in the region (Bailundu and Bié) were fired from their posts. Captain Massano de Amorim, who had led one of the Portuguese columns and served briefly as governor of the district, issued a proclamation. In it he guaranteed both human and personal property rights. The labor codes, which created forced labor, were temporarily suspended, and traders were compelled to live within 15 kilometers (about 9.3 miles) of forts or other government posts so that they could be supervised more closely. The Portuguese established more of such stations so that they could better control the Benguela Highlands.

In spite of these reforms, the Ovimbundu were punished for their actions. Many, including some Ovimbundu leaders, had been killed during the revolt, and afterward the Portuguese government kept closer control of their daily lives. However the Ovimbundu did not think the fight was over. "Despite severe castigation, killing and imprisoning of some of the African Chiefs," observed the writer B. de Almeida, "they did not consider themselves vanquished."

On March 28, 1904, two years after the original revolt had its beginnings, Portuguese troops once more marched through the highlands. During a 12-day campaign, they attacked and were victorious over a group of Ovimbundu who had escaped capture during the first action and were plotting against their Portuguese masters. All the leaders of the Ovimbundu were either dead or arrested, and the people could only look to those appointed by the Portuguese for direction. That same year, the beginning of the construction of the Benguela Railway from the coastal city of Benguela into the interior signaled that another part of Ovimbundu life was coming to an end. When it was completed, their traditional caravans would no longer be needed. To preserve their identity, the Ovimbundu began to emphasize their shared past and to see themselves as a single ethnic group rather than as a collection of small kingdoms.

INTERNATIONAL PROTEST

In the meantime, the Portuguese need for African workers had not ended, and the reforms put in place by Captain Amorim did not last. Soon forced labor was as much a part of Ovimbundu life as it had been since slavery officially ended. Throughout Angola, conditions for *serviçais* did not improve. But for the first time, significant international attention was being placed on the plight of the people of Angola. Part of this was a byproduct of an English-led reform movement directed toward the neighboring Congo Free State where missionaries were reporting horrible atrocities, such as the hacking off of hands and feet. Some of it was motivated by a continuing desire on the part of Britain to gain control of parts of Angola by proving that the Portuguese were an inept colonial power.

Mwata Yamvo Chief, 1910 *A complex of powerful states, under rulers called* Mwata Yamvo, *flourished until the late nineteenth century in the southern Congo basin, eastern Angola, and Zambia. Originally founded by ivory hunters, these Luba-Lunda states became indirectly connected with the Portuguese in Angola. The Portuguese supplied cloth and other goods in return for slaves and ivory. This photograph was taken in 1910 by Mr. T. S. Schindler, who was mapping the Congo-Zambezi watershed.*

Assimilados, those Africans and *mestiços* who had adopted Portuguese customs and language, published a remarkable book in 1901, *The Voice of Angola Crying in the Wilderness: Offered to the Friends of Truth by the Natives.* An anthology of articles written during the previous 11 years against the Portuguese rule in Angola, the 200-page book attacked Portugal's policies in the colony:

> Portugal, having conquered this colony over 400 years ago, has done nothing for the progress of the country, neither in matters material, literary or moral . . . the people are brutalised, as in their former primitive state. . . . This is a crime of outrage against civilisation, leaving this very rich colony stagnant. . . . Only the negligence of its rulers can explain this state of affairs.

The writers went on to say that to them, the civilization offered by Portugal meant "sacking, devastating, selling, torturing, killing." Some Portuguese citizens as well as members of the government were disturbed by such reports coming out of Angola. Judice Biker, a governor of Portuguese Guinea, criticized working conditions and treatment of the *serviçais,* particularly in plantations on the Portuguese island of São Tomé where so many Angolans were shipped. He described 12-hour working days, high infant mortality, poor diet, and the refusal of plantation owners to release workers after they had completed their five-year term of service.

CADBURY'S INSPECTION

Sentiments against Portuguese policy toward Angolans intensified with the 1906 publication of *A Modern Slavery* by Henry W. Nevinson. A famous British journalist of his day, Nevinson confirmed everything Biker had complained about. His work was notable because he criticized the particular individuals responsible for the inhumane treatment while commending those Portuguese who objected to the practices. He suggested that English chocolate manufacturers, such as the Quaker William Cadbury, refuse to buy cocoa from São Tomé.

Cadbury traveled to Lisbon and visited with the new overseas minister, who promised immediate action. Three months later, the minister was replaced. Cadbury corresponded with the Planters' Association. After reviewing the charges placed against plantations on São Tomé and Angola, he warned, "However much it may cost us to leave off buying your excellent cocoa and although we know it will cause a loss . . . we must say that our conscience will not permit us to continue buying the raw material for our industry, if we do not have the certainty of its being produced in the future by a system of free labor." The association claimed that the situation was being misrepresented, so in 1908 Cadbury decided to visit São Tomé and Angola himself.

He published his observations in his book, *Labour in Portuguese West Africa,* along with a similar report made by his employee Joseph Burtt. The latter account described a journey taken into the interior of Angola during the summer of 1906:

> It was not long before we found skeletons and shackles. These shackles are blocks of wood, in which an oblong hole is hewn to admit the hands or feet. A stout peg is then driven through the side, dividing the ankles or wrists, and making withdrawal impossible. . . . In the gully of a dry stream bed, where we stayed to rest, a few yards from where we sat, and under the side of an overhanging rock, we saw the decomposing corpse of a man. Hard by lay a small basket, a large wooden spoon, a native mat, and a few filthy clothes. The dead man lay on his back, with his limbs spread out, probably as he had died, left hopelessly weak by a gang going down to the coast. Another skeleton lay within a few yards, making five we had seen in a few hours' march.

Burtt also recorded the fate of some of the Ovimbundu who had been given letters of freedom after Amorim's reforms and had settled near the fort at Kavungo, sometimes working for the Portuguese officials:

> Then the "commandante" at the fort sent and captured the greater part of the population of this colonial village,

Bridge Across the Catumbela River, Central Angola, c. 1920
In 1965, A hydroelectric plant on the upper Catumbela was com-
pleted. It provides power for the cities of Lobito and Benguela on the
Atlantic coast and for Huambo inland. Huambo, formerly New Lis-
bon, became the headquarters for the UNITA guerrila movement dur-
ing the war for independence.

roped up the women, put the men in chains, and sent them
on their way to the fort at Moshico. . . . The colony at
Kazombo nearly shared the same fate, but the man sent to
take them prematurely stated his errand, and they escaped
before he secured them. On our way to Kavungo we met a
number of people going towards the coast. We were told
they were runaway slaves, and noticed they were in charge
of soldiers armed with chicottes [whips made from hippopotamus hide], rifles, and ammunition. One man who
was seen by one of our party was tied by his hands and
feet, and hung from a pole carried by two men.

Manual Laborers at the São Salvador Mission, 1907 *These men and boys worked for the Reverend Thomas Lewis and his wife at the mission they established in São Salvador. The man standing at the left, wearing a hat, supervised the workers. He had been converted to Christianity.*

Cadbury himself estimated the death rate of laborers on São Tomé from Angola at more than 100 per thousand, based on records kept on large estates. He attributed the high death rate to the methods used in acquiring the workers, the unsanitary living quarters, and crowded living conditions. He also noted that a 10 percent death rate would mean one funeral every week on a large estate.

TURMOIL IN PORTUGAL

External pressure on Portugal about living conditions in Angola and its African islands increased just as internal problems were reaching a flashpoint. For decades, tensions had existed between the aristocracy and commoners, between the

Roman Catholic Church and the intelligentsia. Republicans, as they were called, fought in government to reform a highly stratified society. At times these conflicts led to riots and over-turned governments. In 1907 King Carlos bypassed parliament completely and named his own prime minister. While his goal had been to enact social reforms, the members of parliament were infuriated by his high-handed methods and protested. The king responded by repressing the opposition, and his prime minister created Portugal's first modern dictatorship. As a result, violence increased, and in 1908, King Carlos and his oldest son were assassinated.

In the face of such turmoil at home, the government in Lisbon had little time or money to invest in reforming its colonies. However because many Republican leaders tied their political views with a call for autonomy in Angola, a number of *assimilados* came to believe that a victory by the Republicans in Portugal would mean greater freedom for Angolans.

In practice, however, life in Angola remained unchanged. The governor-general and his forces continued their attempts to achieve effective occupation of the colony. Once the Benguela Highlands had been subdued, they turned their attention to the Kwanyama in southern Angola. Germans in Southwest Africa donated guns to the Kwanyama, who refused to give up. Fighting continued for years without a decisive victory for either side.

To the north, Portuguese officials launched a long and frustrating campaign against the Dembos, a Mbundu group living less than 100 miles northeast of Luanda. Exasperated with abuses by the captains major in their area, the leaders of the Dembos had either killed or chased out the Portuguese appointees. As late as 1907 only a handful of Europeans lived with the Dembos, and they paid high taxes for the privilege. That year, Captain João de Almeida toured the area and determined that he could break the power of its leaders. With the assistance of 1,000 men obtained from the governor-general, he began a series of skirmishes against one village after another. Within three years, the Dembos were largely subdued, although pockets of resistance continued to exist well into the next decade.

Market, Kongo Province, c. 1905 *In the Kongo Province at the turn of the twentieth century, there were four market days:* konzo, nkenge, nsona, *and* nkandu. *These markets gave their names to the four main days that make up the Kongo week. Markets held on a certain day all over the Kongo are called* konzo, *and the markets held the next day are named* nkenge, *and so on. Every village in the province had within reasonable walking distance at least one weekly market where goods could be bartered.*

In 1910 the political conflict in Portugal resulted in the late King Carlos's youngest son being forced from the country. The Republicans seized control of the government and proclaimed Portugal a Republic. When news of these events reached Luanda, *assimilados* felt hope for the first time that significant reforms might finally be realized in Angola. It remained to be seen, however, if the promises of autonomy for Angola that Republicans had made would become a reality.

San (Bushmen), 1923 *The San (Bushmen) are an indigenous people of southern Africa. They live by hunting and foraging and are virtually untouched by the outside world. For hunting, they use bows and poisoned arrows, snares, and spears. Colonel John C. B. Statham described meeting the San group in this photograph: "We saw their little encampment of a mat or two under a temporary leaf shelter, where they had stopped to eat a kudu [a large African antelope], wounded with a poisoned arrow, and then tracked for miles to where it died, and the family camped."*

9

SECOND~CLASS CITIZENS

When news of the October 1910 overthrow of the Portuguese monarchy and the establishment of the Portuguese Republic reached Luanda, most *assimilados* were ecstatic. Perhaps at long last steps could be taken to change the role of Africans in Angola. Learning that poor children in Portugal were finally being given schooling encouraged them further. Such a policy could be extended to Portugal's colonies, where the lack of education for African children prevented them from participating in the colony's government.

Assimilados had another reason for wanting more education to be available. Many of them worked in Luanda and Benguela in government jobs. But the mission schools and the few government schools that were available did not provide education beyond the fifth grade. It soon became clear that one of the aims of the new government in Portugal was to change the way its colonies were run. Rather than relying on military officers to represent the government in interior outposts, Portugal wanted to use civilian government employees. It established a school in Lisbon to train such workers. But it also changed the requirements for employment in government jobs. Workers would have to have at least a secondary school education, something that wasn't offered in Angola. Many *assimilados* wondered what would happen to their jobs as the educational standards changed.

MIRANDA'S MARCH

Before such action could become standard policy, an *assimilado* named António Joaquim de Miranda decided to take action. Born in 1864, Miranda had received an education, and at age 21 he took a job as a clerk at a plantation. He worked there for the next 20 years, and during journeys he took into the interior of Angola, he became aware of the cruel treatment handed out to African workers. In 1908 he quit his job and wrote to the governor-general, objecting to the abuses he had witnessed. Perhaps because so many other sources were criticizing Angolan labor policy at the same time, Miranda didn't suffer for making his concerns known. A short while later, he became a public employee in Luanda.

After the monarchy was overthrown in Portugal, Miranda organized a group called Education for the People—Mutual Assistance. They created a petition calling for specific reforms in Angolan public education. On March 12, 1911, hundreds of people led by Miranda peacefully marched to the home of Governor-General Manual Maria Coêlho and presented him with a copy of the petition. What stood out to witnesses was that almost all the marchers were African. They were holding the first demonstration by an African group to call for reforms from the Portuguese government.

Coêlho greeted the marchers courteously and accepted their recommendations. Much to their disappointment, however, over the next several months no action was taken. Within a year, Miranda was transferred 250 miles into the interior to act as tax collector. In this way, the government quietly denied the Africans' request.

INSTITUTIONALIZED RACISM

Lack of action by the government wasn't simply the result of both Portugal and Angola having financial problems. Portuguese attitudes toward Africans were hardening. Some Portuguese were attracted to German ideas of racial superiority. Those ideas validated centuries of Portuguese behavior toward Africans both in Angola and in Portugal. By 1912 the new governor-general of Angola, Norton de Matos, explained race relations in Angola with these words:

> Respect and affection for the man of color rapidly disappeared, we began to have reluctance in considering him our equal, we were left with the belief that a black could never fully attain our civilization, to be intellectually, morally, politically, and socially equal to us.

Assimilado fears that they would be cut off from access to government jobs soon became reality. In 1913 administrators, secretaries, and clerks needed for the local government in Angola were appointed back in Lisbon. The next year brought demands for a double standard in pay. "In the majority of cases the black employee *cannot* in good justice, working alongside whites, receive the same salary," went the argument.

Those Africans who were not part of the Angolan governing structure faced their own problems as the decade began. The rubber trade, which for so long had been a major source of work and income, was dying. Mature rubber plantations in South America, the East Indies, and on the African west coast supplied a consistently high quality product. Rubber from Angola was rated "third class" and sold at one-fourth its former rate.

For the Ovimbundu, the rubber trade essentially ended in 1911, remembered as "the year of the great hunger in the Ngangela country." At the beginnning of the dry season, caravans started out on their traditional routes, carrying enough food with them to get through the "hungry country," as a stretch of forest where there were no settlements was called. After that, they would reach villages where they expected to be able to trade for food. But a drought had hit the villages on the other side of the hungry country. There was no food available for trade. Some Ovimbundu in desperation ate wax and later died. A few resorted to cannibalism on the principle that it was better for at least one brother to return than for both to starve. Most of the caravans simply disappeared. The few people who managed to return to the highlands looked like skeletons.

In spite of the drop in rubber trade, demand for forced labor had not decreased. Cocoa, sugar, and cotton plantations created a continuing need for more workers, and the government was immersed in large public works projects, building roads and the Benguela Railroad. Significant reforms in labor laws were passed in Lisbon, however there wasn't enough money to enforce them and landowners refused to abide by them, in any event.

With the decrease in trade, however, mission schools began seeing higher attendance. In all areas of the country, Protestant missionaries were teaching children how to read and write in their own language. Most Protestant missionaries were English-speaking and had little desire to learn Portuguese as well as the language of whichever African group they were living with. In contrast, Roman Catholic missionaries placed an emphasis on Portuguese because of their historical and financial ties to Portugal. Because of their dependency on the strained Portuguese treasury, Roman Catholic missions were often understaffed and in need of equipment. The Protestants were supported by mission agencies, usually from North America. With greater and more reliable funding they had better access to medical and

Mrs. Statham and Bamangando, the Rainmaker, 1923 *This rainmaker, photographed with the wife of explorer John C. B. Statham, was also a leading Mambukushu chief. Allegedly, before calling for rain, the chief drank a potion that contained the blood of an infant killed for that purpose. Note that he is wearing Mrs. Statham's jacket.*

The Stathams met the Mambukushu along the Kubango River in southeast Angola, about fifteen miles before the river forms part of the Angola-Namibia border. The male Mambukushu had their hair cut short and shaved over the forehead. The women wore their hair in long pigtails that contained beads and small ostrich bones. Both men and women wore animal skins or cloth drawn between their legs and tied around the waist.

school supplies and placed a priority on introducing Western medical practices and education as well as Christianity to the Africans.

Government plans increasingly conflicted with mission-school ideals. In 1914, the Department of Native Affairs was established in Angola. It was responsible for everything that had anything to do with Angolans, including education. The first head of this department, José de Oliveira Ferreira Dinis, wanted schools to be more workshops than centers of education. Believing that Africans were greatly inferior to the Portuguese, he felt they could be best served by schools that gave them minimal vocational training and helped them become better manual workers.

The government also began to crack down on signs of independent thought among Africans. Miranda, the *assimilado* promoter of education, was fired from his government job. Charged with forming a secret political society and trying to overthrow Portuguese rule in Angola, he was exiled.

Concerns about Portuguese control of Angola shot up the next year when Germany invaded southern Angola from its colony of Southwest Africa. In the process of driving the Germans out of Angola during 1915, the Portuguese finally succeeded in suppressing most of the Kwanyama in the region. They also were thrown ill-prepared into World War I and racked up massive debts before the war was over.

Mambukushu Women, 1923 *These two women were photographed beside a canoe. All Mambukushu were expected to be expert canoers. Their main village is an island in the Kubango River surrounded by rapids on every side. The river, which runs up and down for 20–30 miles, is rock-strewn, and the current is so swift as to be extremely dangerous to navigate.*

Colonel John C. B. Statham wrote that to see the Mambukushu "standing up in their canoes, plying their long pole-like paddles, and to watch them balancing long slender canoes with almost effortless grace, is to admire unpleasant people in spite of oneself."

The First World War did not help Portugal's Republican government gain stability. In 16 years of power, the Republicans went through 44 governments and had only one president serve his full term. As the 1920s approached, the government became increasingly committed to the idea of creating political unity in order to establish economic and social stability. In Angola, that policy translated into more forceful repression of anything non-Portuguese. Increasing numbers of *assimilados* were arrested on trumped-up charges and began taking to heart an African proverb that "The black can never be right."

REPRESSION UNDER MATOS

Repression reached a new height in 1921 when Norton de Matos became high commissioner of Angola, a post that had replaced governor-general. This was his second term as head of Angola, and he was determined to impose Portuguese oversight on all of the colony. To begin with, the structure of government was changed. Angola was divided into 11 administrative districts. Each large district was divided into 65 smaller parts, each headed by an administrator. With very few exceptions, these officials were white.

The high commissioner also spent huge amounts of money creating more roads and continuing work on the Benguela railroad. He wanted Portuguese officials to have improved access throughout the colony and also wanted to establish Portuguese communities in the highlands. These improvement projects cost more money than the colony had available. Matos benefited from the income generated by the newly created Diamond Company of Angola, but the government still needed more income. Driven to creating economic stability in the colony, he raised taxes on all Angolans. These increases hit the people just when the colony was suffering economic hard times. In some cases, local administrators listed underage boys as adults on the tax roles so that they could increase income from their district.

Matos also attacked problems he believed were caused by non-Portuguese foreigners. He passed laws that limited land-holding by Boers from South Africa. Passport restrictions and immigration controls were tightened in an effort to crush the German presence in the colony.

Matos was determined to squelch African identity. He recognized that Protestant missionaries were encouraging such identity by teaching African groups to read and write in their own languages. Decree 77, passed in 1921, made the teaching and printing of these languages in mission schools illegal. It also required that teachers hold certificates of proficiency to teach Portuguese, something few Protestant missionaries possessed. Robert Graham, a Baptist missionary in northern Angola, described the effect of Decree 77:

> This meant the closing of over two hundred of our little village schools, where the children were being taught to read the Scriptures in their native tongue; thus cutting the sinew of this very important branch of our work, and condemning thousands of native children to illiteracy and ignorance; for we could not provide, and the Government would not provide, the towns with Portuguese teachers.

As a further step in asserting Portuguese dominance, Matos banned African associations and closed down independent newspapers and other publishing ventures in Luanda. These actions were designed to suppress *assimilado* efforts to gain African rights and an end to forced labor. Several dozen *assimilado* leaders were exiled. Others were thrown in Luanda jails.

By 1926 Matos and the high commissioners who followed him had succeeded in either imprisoning or exiling any known *assimilados* who appeared to favor African rule in Angola. Those *assimilados* who remained in government understood clearly the consequences of speaking out against the Portuguese way of doing things.

In May of that same year, Roman Catholic soldiers toppled the last Republican government in Portugal. This military coup led to what became known as the New State. For many Portuguese in Angola, the New State meant more power. What they failed to notice was that the dream of independence had not died in the hearts of the people they continued to exploit.

Angolan Chief, C.1930

10

THE PRICE OF FREEDOM

Since many of the problems that had brought down the republican government in Portugal were economic, it was not surprising that the most important person in the new single-party government of Portugal was a young professor of economics named António de Oliveira Salazar. Salazar was appointed minister of finance in 1928, and it was soon clear that he intended to reorganize the finances of Portugal by drastically decreasing expenditures on government programs at home and by uniting the economies of Portugal and its colonies to form one large economic system. He believed that Angola could become a protected market for Portuguese wines, textiles, and other manufactured goods. At the same time, the colony could supply Portugal with important agricultural products such as coffee, sugar, and cotton. The development of natural resources such as oil, diamonds, and mineral deposits was also an important part of his plan. These commodities would not only provide raw materials for Portuguese industry, but they would also generate wealth through exports to other parts of the industrialized world.

THE NEW STATE

By the time Salazar was appointed Minister of Colonies in 1930, he had become a virtual dictator, and the Colonial Act of that year put into effect his plans for the exploitation of Portugal's overseas empire. When he became prime minister in 1932, he was the most powerful man in Portugal. The new Portuguese constitution of 1933 made the racist and authoritarian principles of his New State the law of all Portuguese lands—including Angola. Though Salazar's plans for Angola were economic, the most important changes they brought to those who lived there were social and political.

New laws limited the bureaucratic level to which *mestiços* and *assimilados* could rise, established different pay scales for Europeans and non-Europeans, and restricted competition between them for jobs. These laws created hard feelings among *mestiços,* who had until this point tended to identify with whites rather than with Africans.

Even more sinister was the change that came over the way all Angolans were viewed. Portugal previously had assumed that Africans would somehow be assimilated into European society, but the New State established exacting standards that Africans had to meet to qualify for citizens' rights. Laws passed between 1926 and 1933 defined Africans as a separate element in the population, referred to as ***indígenas.*** Those who learned to speak Portuguese, who took jobs in commerce or industry, and who behaved as Portuguese citizens were classified as *assimilados.* In accepting the rights of citizenship, *assimilados* took on the same tax obligations as European citizens. Male *indígenas* were required to pay a head tax. If they could not raise the money, they were obligated to work for the government for half of each year without wages. Other repressive measures continued in the new government, including forced labor practices, repression of nationalist activities, and severe press censorship.

NATIONAL INTEGRATION

Portugal's policies toward Angola in the 1930s and 1940s were based on the principle of national integration. Angola was to become an integral part of the Portuguese nation. In line with these policies, Portugal renamed African towns, usually after Portuguese heroes. A few years later, Portugal withdrew the currency known as the *angolar* and replaced it with the Portuguese *escudo.*

Angolan Chief and Family, C. 1930
By 1920, all but the remote southeast part of Angola was firmly under Portugese control. Kingdoms were abolished and the Portugese worked directly through chiefs. These chiefs served primarily as "errandboys" for the local Portugese administrator. Rarely did they express some of the feelings and desires of the people.

Portugal sought to make Angola self-supporting and to turn it into a market for Portuguese goods. But despite a certain degree of success, Angola enjoyed no real prosperity until after World War II, when higher coffee prices brought enormous profits to Angolan producers—who were primarily newly arrived Portuguese settlers. It was also at this time that the Portuguese government encouraged its poor rural residents to move to Angola. They were given land and jobs that the colonial government seized from Africans.

Beginning in the 1940s, the system of forced labor came under renewed criticism. One particularly outspoken critic, Captain Henrique Galvão, had served as a government official for more than two decades in Angola. He chronicled abuses

Angolan Dancers, Along the Kwanza River, c. 1928 *This remarkable photograph is of Angolan tribal dancers and Mrs. Frank Varian. The Varians were among the very few long-term English residents in Angola. They lived in the inland town of Huambo, which lies south of the Kwanza River. Mr. Varian was the chief construction engineer for the Benguela Railway, which extended from Lobito on the coast to the Congolese border.*

committed against the African population. He noted that the government was so desperate for workers that, "to cover the deficit the most shameful outrages are committed, including forced labour of independent self-employed workers, of women, of children, of the sick, of decrepit old men, etc. *Only the dead are really exempt from forced labour."*

The Salazar government responded by arresting Galvão for treason and banning his report. Despite the introduction of some labor reforms from the late 1940s through the late 1950s, forced labor continued.

In 1950, of an estimated 4 million Africans in Angola, fewer than 31,000 were *assimilados* with the rights of citizens. To help it more easily control the millions of *indígenas,* the colonial government required them to carry identification cards. The authoritarian Salazar regime frequently used African informants to ferret out signs of political opposition. Censorship, border control, police action, and repressive educational policies were used to prevent, or at least slow, the development of African leaders. Africans studying in Portugal—and therefore exposed to "progressive" ideas—were sometimes prevented from returning to Angola. Political offenses brought severe penalties. Some early nationalist organizations were abolished, while others were transformed into government-approved cultural societies.

RESISTANCE MOVEMENTS

In spite of government opposition, two major nationalist movements rose up during the 1950s. The Popular Movement for the Liberation of Angola (MPLA) was created in Luanda in December 1956. Its aim was to achieve independence by presenting a united front for all African interests. It held strong Marxist-Leninist beliefs and gained a reputation for representing the interests of urban intellectuals rather than ordinary Angolans throughout the country. The majority of its members came from the Mbundu. Because of its communist philosophies, the MPLA gained support from both the Soviet Union and China. They saw Angola as a potential beachhead for a Marxist-Leninist presence in Africa.

The National Front for the Liberation of Angola (FNLA) also had its roots in the 1950s. At that time, two smaller Angolan organizations sought the restoration of the Kongo Kingdom and worked with the Alliance of Bakongo (Abako) in what was then the Belgian Congo to achieve this goal. It quickly became clear that the Kongo Kingdom would not be reborn, and the two Angolan groups combined in 1962 to form the FNLA. Although its leadership represented many ethnic groups, the followers remained largely Kongo. It received aid from the United States through the CIA.

At first, these groups were disorganized, lacking strong leadership. Many of the leaders were used to thinking in terms of ethnic interests rather than considering the well-being of Angola as a whole. And while many members of the white community wanted to break away from Portugal, they also wanted to maintain the colonial nature of Angola's government.

STRUGGLE FOR INDEPENDENCE

But Angolans noticed their African neighbors gaining independence from colonial powers, and at the same time, the Portuguese became increasingly repressive. By 1961 tensions had reached a breaking point. A group of rebels attacked police stations and prisons, hoping to free political prisoners. Cotton workers took on government officials and buildings, as well as a Catholic mission. In the northwest, Kongo raided isolated farms and towns, killing hundreds of Europeans. Settlers responded by forming vigilante committees that killed and terrorized Africans, destroying their crops. When the 1961 uprisings were over, as many as 40,000 Africans had died through violence, disease, or famine, and about 400 Europeans were killed. Wealthy white settlers left the country, leaving only poor whites and members of the military and government behind.

Over the next 14 years, the MPLA and the FNLA developed military organizations intent on overthrowing the Portuguese

Along the Zambezi River, C. 1930
*The Zambezi River drains a large portion of south-central Africa.
Together with its tributaries, it forms the fourth largest river basin of
the continent.*

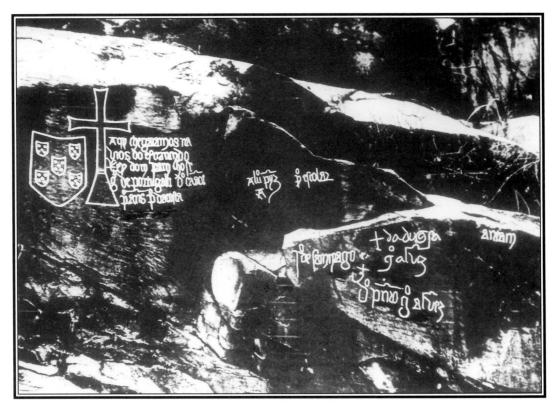

Diogo Cão Rock Inscription, Near Matadi, 1482 *Between 1482 and 1484, the Portuguese explorer Diogo Cão explored the coast of what is now Gabon, the Congo, and most of Angola. Since Cão had been instructed to investigate any possible water passage across Africa, he sailed almost 60 miles up the Congo River. Near the present city of Matadi, his men went ashore and placed a monument with this inscription: "In the 6681st year of the creation of the world and the 1,482nd year of the birth of Our Lord Jesus Christ, the very high, excellent and powerful ruler, King John II of Portugal, ordered this land be discovered and these monuments placed by Diogo Cão, squire of his house."*

Near the site of the monument, Cão had his men carve into hard rock the Portuguese coat of arms, a representation of Cão's monument, and this inscription: "Here arrived the ships of King John II of Portugal." Then follows the name of Diogo Cão and those of several of his crew to the right. This photograph is of the rock inscription.

When Cão became the first European to reach the Congo River, he also became the first European to learn of the vast Kingdom of the Kongo. By the middle of the fifteenth century, the ManiKongo (Kongo king) ruled what is now northern Angola and most of present day Congo (Zaire). Farther down the Atlantic coast, Cão made peaceful contact with the people of Ndongo, whose kingdom extended inland from Luanda. Their ruler was called the ngola. *The pronunciation became "Angola," by which word the Portuguese referred to the entire area.*

colonial government. In 1966 the fight was joined by a third group, the National Union for the Total Independence of Angola (UNITA). Headed by Jonas Savimbi, UNITA was made up of Ovimbundu, Angolan students from abroad, and Angolan refugees in Zambia. Because it couldn't get support from other African nations or from the Soviet Union, UNITA accepted military aid and training from the Chinese.

As the war continued, divisions developed among the three nationalist groups. Portugal exploited the situation, and by the early 1970s most of the rebels had been forced out of the country. But the drain on Portugal's treasury increased. It was also fighting wars in its other African territories. By 1974, 11,000 Portuguese military personnel had died in Africa. On April 25, 1974, the military overthrew the Portuguese government and quickly moved to grant the African territories independence.

As the Portuguese began releasing Angolan political prisoners, whites in Angola became terrified. In July rioting broke out in Luanda, with whites massacring African slum dwellers and pillaging homes and businesses. The Portuguese army quickly put the riot down, but the problems had only begun. Portugal attempted to form a united Angolan government, but the three nationalist groups were unable to work together. The provisional government quickly fell apart, and Angola plunged into civil war.

Civil War

By March 1976 the MPLA controlled of much of Angola, largely because of assistance from the Soviet Union, Eastern Europe, and Cuba. FNLA members were in exile, and UNITA was largely held to eastern and southwestern Angola, from where it launched guerilla raids against the government. UNITA received help from South Africa because the MPLA was supporting the Namibian independence movement in that nation. Meanwhile, the MPLA crushed a coup attempt, eliminated any perceived opposition, and officially became a Marxist-Leninist party. It quickly converted the economy along communist ideals with disastrous results. Only the rapidly growing oil industry, managed by foreign companies, prevented complete economic and military collapse. In 1979 José Eduardo dos Santos was appointed president upon the death of President Agostinho Neto.

In 1985 the United States began giving military aid to UNITA through Zaire. Soon the whole country was being ripped apart by fighting. But in 1988 South Africa agreed to Namibian independence and withdrew its support from UNITA. Then the Cubans agreed to withdraw from Angola. Faced with the loss of outside aid, both the MPLA and UNITA agreed to a cease-fire in 1989. The peace agreement did not last, but those within the MPLA who were working for peace gained more power because of the collapse of communism in Eastern Europe.

The 1990s began with hopeful signs. The collapse of the Soviet Union and the discrediting of communist economic theories gave further impetus to the MPLA's work on the Angolan economy. By mid-1990, the MPLA Central Committee had decided to formally abandon both Marxism-Leninism and the security of a one-party state.

With the effective end of the Cold War, the nations that had encouraged the conflict between UNITA and the MPLA were withdrew from Angola. After a final ill-conceived, costly, and unsuccessful attempt to crush UNITA, the dos Santos government decided to negotiate with its enemies. By May 1991, the two sides had again agreed to a cease-fire. They also made commitments to a new national constitution which guaranteed both political and human rights to everyone in Angola. Multiparty elections were scheduled for September 1992. But after the MPLA won those elections, Jonas Savimbi and UNITA returned to the battlefield.

Throughout the winter and spring, fighting continued, with both sides claiming important victories. Attempts to begin talks leading to a new cease fire failed because of UNITA's refusal to withdraw from areas it had occupied. In May 1993 the United States officially recognized the government of President José dos Santos. Attempts to get humanitarian aid to victims of the fighting in several parts of the country were blocked by UNITA. By that fall, the number of persons displaced by the conflict reached 2 million, nearly one-fifth the entire population of Angola.

In November 1993 peace talks between the dos Santos government and UNITA began in Lusaka, Zambia. While the talks continued, fighting escalated on many fronts. The tragic effects of the continuing war on the people of Angola were starkly summarized by a single line from the proposed 1994 budget, in which military spending was by far the largest item. The finance minister stated that he hoped to lower the annual inflation rate to 260 percent by the end of 1994. At the end of 1993 it had been 1,840 percent.

Peace talks broke off late in the summer of 1994, but on November 20, UN negotiators reported that they had patched together a deal between the warring parties. It became known as the Lusaka Accords.

A Devastated Nation

Aid agencies were faced with a formidable task. The World Food Programme alone earmarked $65 million to help 1.2 million displaced persons, refugees, and demobilized soldiers in areas where there was an acute shortage of food. On February 8, 1995, the UN Security Council resolved to send a 7,000-member peacekeeping force to monitor developments. Among their tasks was the dangerous job of helping to remove an estimated 10 million to 15 million land mines.

UNITA leader Jonas Savimbi agreed to meet dos Santos. The two men met in Lusaka on May 6, 1995. Their discussions resulted in a vote by the National Assembly to amend the constitution to provide for the creation of two vice presidential posts, one of which would be filled by Savimbi. UNITA would then become a political party and would be offered ministerial posts in a power-sharing government, but there would be no presidential election until the expiration of dos Santos's term. Savimbi declared himself willing to act as vice president and said his party would accept the ministerial appointments offered. UNITA remained nervous, however, about the new national army, charging it with brutality toward those living in regions UNITA had formerly controlled.

Other nations encouraged the peace process. South Africa agreed to help develop Angola's oil and diamond resources.

Portugal agreed to train a national police force. Altogether, still other nations offered $1 billion in aid. Serious problems remained, however. Rampant inflation made food, furniture, household appliances, clothing, and medical care unaffordable for most Angolans. Hopes of recovery were further diminished in 1996, when UNITA fell behind on the schedule for troop demobilization. Because of these delays, the UN Security Council decided to shorten the time its peacekeeping forces would be stationed in Angola.

Then Savimbi refused to accept the office of vice president because it gave him no real power. Disputes also arose over control of the important diamond-producing provinces in eastern Angola, which were deep inside UNITA territory. Throughout the next two years, the peace process lurched along. Then in July 1998 more than 200 people in the diamond-mining province of Lunda Norte were massacred. The government and UNITA accused each other of responsibility for the killings. Soon civil war engulfed Angola again.

On February 26, 1999, the UN Security Council, acting on the recommendation of UN Secretary-General Kofi Annan, voted unanimously to disband its peacekeeping mission. It also placed more severe sanctions on sales of arms to UNITA and on diamond purchases from UNITA-controlled mines, long a source of funds for UNITA's military operations. These sanctions have gradually weakened UNITA's ability to wage war and strengthened the position of the MPLA government. The Angolan government is once again considering political solutions to what in essence has been a 25-year civil war. It may offer amnesty to members of UNITA, including Jonas Savimbi.

Since 1975 warfare has killed 2 million people in Angola and displaced 4 million more. There are 400,000 orphans, and hundreds of thousands of people have been injured. Millions of landmines continue to threaten public safety and place severe restrictions on both travel and farming. Schools and medical clinics have been destroyed, and companies are reluctant to risk

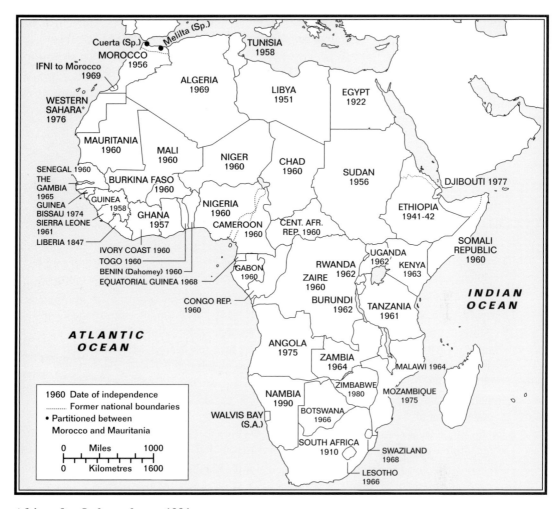

Africa after Independence, 1991

investing in a devastated economy. The increasing AIDS epidemic on the African continent and other untreated diseases threaten to further destabilize Angolan society. It remains to be seen how long it will take for Angola to benefit from its wealth in both natural and human resources.

GLOSSARY

assimilados—originally referred to Africans and *mestiços* who had adopted Portuguese customs and language. In 1933 it became a legal term defining people who had met a rigorous standard for citizenship in Angola.

camara—title given to the town council of Luanda that replaced the governor-general whenever he was absent from the colony.

chicotte—a whip made from hippopotamus hide and used to beat slaves. It ripped the flesh open and often killed people.

degradados—people convicted of serious crimes such as homicide and theft in Portugal and sent to Angola as part of their punishment.

forced labor—a policy that allowed Europeans to force Africans into labor if they were "vagrants," a term defined as men not working for Europeans or their agents. Forced labor created a legal slavery.

indígenas—title given to Africans under a series of repressive laws passed between 1926 and 1933.

libertos—title given to freed slaves who were still expected to work for their masters, although theoretically they were protected from physical abuse and guaranteed payment.

mestiços—people of both Portuguese and African ancestry.

Padroado—agreement between the Holy Ghost Fathers and the Portuguese government that outlined responsibilities of both groups to the mission work in Angola.

palmatorio—a thick wooden paddle with small holes that was slapped against the palm of an offender's hand several times, sucking the flesh up through the holes and forming painful welts.

pombeiros—name originally given to slave traders in Angola and later used as a more general term for all traders.

presidio—a division of Angola that was headed by a military commander who had absolute authority.

sertanejo—title given to backwoodsmen famous for their skills in exploration and knowledge of the interior of Angola.

serviçais—name given to contract employees who were forced to work in conditions resembling slavery under a series of labor laws.

soba—name of leader of an Ovimbundu kingdom.

CHRONOLOGY

1878 Native Labor Code outlaws slavery in Angola but creates "forced labor" for Africans not already working for Europeans or their agents; Serpa Pinto begins expedition across Africa

1881 *How I Crossed Africa* by Serpa Pinto is published in Portuguese and English; Serpa Pinto is hailed as national hero

1885 Berlin Conference concludes; principle of "effective occupation" is established as standard by which colonization of areas will be allowed to continue; William Taylor's self-supporting mission group arrives in Luanda

1890 Silva Porto commits suicide; Portuguese military begins occupation of Benguela Highlands

1891 King Ndunduma is captured and exiled; Portuguese select his replacement

1894 Heli Chatelain publishes *Folk-Tales of Angola: Fifty Tales, with Ki-Mbundu Text, Literal English Translation, Introduction, and Notes*

1901 Publication of *The Voice of Angola Crying in the Wilderness: Offered to the Friends of Truth by the Natives,* an anthology of articles written by Angolans during the previous 11 years against Portuguese rule

1902 Bailundu Revolt leads to temporary reforms in labor laws

1904 Effective occupation of Benguela Highlands achieved; construction of Benguela Railroad begins

1906 Publication of *A Modern Slavery* by Henry W. Nevinson increases international opposition to Portuguese policy in Angola

1908 King Carlos of Portugal and his oldest son are assassinated

1909 William Cadbury, British chocolatier and Quaker, publishes *Labour in Portuguese West Africa* and calls for a boycott of cocoa from São Tomé

1910 Portuguese monarchy is overthrown and replaced by Portuguese Republic

1911 First African demonstration to request changes in Portuguese policy in Angola is held in Luanda; led by António Joaquim de Miranda

1915 Portugal enters World War I and substantially completes effective occupation of Angola

1921 Norton de Matos becomes high commissioner of Angola; passes several laws to repress opposition to Portuguese rule, including Decree 77 which outlaws teaching or publishing in African languages

1926 Opposition *assimilados* are either exiled or jailed; Portuguese Republic is overthrown in military coup and replaced by the New State

CHRONOLOGY

1933   New Portuguese constitution makes racist policies of New State the law of the land for Angola; new laws increasingly limit African movement and legal rights

1950s   Nationalist movements including the MPLA and FNLA begin to develop

1961   Major uprisings leave 40,000 Africans dead and cause wealthy Portuguese to leave Angola

1974   Military coup in Portugal overthrows government; Angola is granted independence; civil war begins

1976   MPLA controls most of Angola; civil war with UNITA continues

1993   The United States officially recognizes the government of President José dos Santos, the leader of the MPLA; UNITA enters peace talks with the Angola government

2000   Continuing sanctions and international pressure decrease UNITA's ability to wage war; the MPLA once again considers political solutions to the 25-year-old civil war

WORLD WITHOUT END

DEIRDRE SHIELDS

ONE SUMMER'S DAY in 1830, a group of Englishmen met in London and decided to start a learned society to promote "that most important and entertaining branch of knowledge—Geography," and the Royal Geographical Society (RGS) was born.

The society was formed by the Raleigh Travellers' Club, an exclusive dining club, whose members met over exotic meals to swap tales of their travels. Members included Lord Broughton, who had travelled with the poet Byron, and John Barrow, who had worked in the iron foundries of Liverpool before becoming a force in the British Admiralty.

From the start, the Royal Geographical Society led the world in exploration, acting as patron and inspiration for the great expeditions to Africa, the Poles, and the Northwest Passage, that elusive sea connection between the Atlantic and Pacific. In the scramble to map the world, the society embodied the spirit of the age: that English exploration was a form of benign conquest.

The society's gold medal awards for feats of exploration read like a Who's Who of famous explorers, among them David Livingstone, for his 1855 explorations in Africa; the American explorer Robert Peary, for his 1898 discovery of the "northern termination of the Greenland ice"; Captain Robert Scott, the first Englishman to reach the South Pole, in 1912; and on and on.

Today the society's headquarters, housed in a red-brick Victorian lodge in South Kensington, still has the effect of a gentleman's club, with courteous staff, polished wood floors, and fine paintings.

Angola

The building archives the world's most important collection of private exploration papers, maps, documents, and artefacts. Among the RGS's treasures are the hats Livingstone and Henry Morton Stanley wore at their famous meeting ("Dr. Livingstone, I presume?") at Ujiji in 1871, and the chair the dying Livingstone was carried on during his final days in Zambia. The collection also includes models of expedition ships, paintings, dug-out canoes, polar equipment, and Charles Darwin's pocket sextant.

The library's 500,000 images cover the great moments of exploration. Here is Edmund Hillary's shot of Sherpa Tenzing standing on Everest. Here is Captain Lawrence Oates, who deliberately walked out of his tent in a blizzard to his death because his illness threatened to delay Captain Scott's party. Here, too is the American Museum of Natural History's 1920 expedition across the Gobi Desert in dusty convoy (the first to drive motorised vehicles across a desert).

The day I visited, curator Francis Herbert was trying to find maps for five different groups of adventurers at the same time from the largest private map collection in the world. Among the 900,000 items are maps dating to 1482 and ones showing the geology of the moon and thickness of ice in Antarctica, star atlases, and "secret" topographic maps from the former Soviet Union.

The mountaineer John Hunt pitched a type of base camp in a room at the RGS when he organised the 1953 Everest expedition that put Hillary and Tenzing on top of the world. "The society was my base, and source of my encouragement," said the late Lord Hunt, who noted that the nature of that work is different today from what it was when he was the society's president from 1976 to 1980. "When I was involved, there was still a lot of genuine territorial exploration to be done. Now, virtually every important corner—of the land surface, at any rate—has been discovered, and exploration has become more a matter of detail, filling in the big picture."

The RGS has shifted from filling in blanks on maps to providing a lead for the new kind of exploration, under the banner of geography: "I see exploration not so much as a question of 'what' and 'where' anymore, but 'why' and 'how': How does the earth work, the environment function, and how do we manage our resources sustainably?" says the society's director, Dr. Rita Gardner. "Our role today is to answer such questions at the senior level of scientific research," Gardner continues, "through our big, multidisciplinary expeditions, through the smaller expeditions we support and encourage, and by advancing the subject of geography, advising governments, and encouraging wider public understanding. Geography is the subject of the 21st century because it embraces everything—peoples, cultures, landscapes, environments—and pulls them all together."

The society occupies a unique position in world-class exploration. To be invited to speak at the RGS is still regarded as an accolade, the ultimate seal of approval of Swan, who in 1989 became the first person to walk to both the North and South Poles, and who says, "The hairs still stand on the back of my neck when I think about the first time I spoke at the RGS. It was the greatest honour."

The RGS set Swan on the path of his career as an explorer, assisting him with a 1979 expedition retracing Scott's journey to the South Pole. "I was a Mr. Nobody, trying to raise seven million dollars, and getting nowhere," says Swan. "The RGS didn't tell me I was mad—they gave me access to Scott's private papers. From those, I found fifty sponsors who had supported Scott, and persuaded them to fund me. On the basis of a photograph I found of one of his chaps sitting on a box of 'Shell Spirit,' I got Shell to sponsor the fuel for my ship."

The name "Royal Geographical Society" continues to open doors. Although the society's actual membership—some 12,600 "fellows," as they are called—is small, the organisation offers an incomparable network of people, experience, and expertise. This is seen in the work of the Expeditionary Advisory Centre. The EAC was established in 1980 to provide a focus for would-be explorers. If you want to know how to raise sponsorship, handle snakes safely, or find a mechanic for your trip across the Sahara, the EAC can help. Based in Lord Hunt's old Everest office, the EAC funds some 50 small expeditions a year and offers practical training and advice to hundreds more. Its safety tips range from the pragmatic—"In subzero temperatures, metal spectacle frames can cause frostbite (as can earrings and nose-rings)"—to the unnerving—"Remember: A decapitated snake head can still bite."

The EAC is unique, since it is the only centre in the world that helps small-team, low-budget expeditions, thus keeping the amateur—in the best sense of the word—tradition of exploration alive.

"The U.K. still sends out more small expeditions per capita than any other country," says Dr. John Hemming, director of the RGS from 1975 to 1996. During his tenure, Hemming witnessed the growth in exploration-travel. "In the 1960s we'd be dealing with 30 to 40 expeditions a year. By 1997 it was 120, but the quality hadn't gone down—it had gone up. It's a boom time for exploration, and the RGS is right at the heart of it."

While the EAC helps adventure-travellers, it concentrates its funding on scientific field research projects, mostly at the university level. Current projects range from studying the effect of the pet trade on Madagscar's chameleons, to mapping uncharted terrain in the south Ecuadorian cloud forest. Jen Hurst is a typical "graduate" of the EAC. With two fellow Oxford students, she received EAC technical training, support, and a $2,000 grant to do biological surveys in the Kyabobo Range, a new national park in Ghana.

"The RGS's criteria for funding are very strict," says Hurst. "They put you through a real grilling, once you've made your application. They're very tough on safety, and very keen on working alongside people from the host country. The first thing they wanted to be sure of was whether we would involve local students. They're the leaders of good practice in the research field."

When Hurst and her colleagues returned from Ghana in 1994, they presented a case study of their work at an EAC seminar. Their talk prompted a $15,000 award from the BP oil company for them to set up a registered charity, the Kyabobo Conservation Project, to ensure that work in the park continues, and that followup ideas for community-based conservation, social, and education projects are developed. "It's been a great experience, and crucial to the careers we hope to make in environmental work," says Hurst. "And it all started through the RGS."

The RGS is rich in prestige but it is not particularly wealthy in financial terms. Compared to the National Geographic Society in the U.S., the RGS is a pauper. However, bolstered by sponsorship from such companies as British Airways and Discovery Channel Europe, the RGS remains one of Britain's largest organisers of geographical field research overseas.

The ten major projects the society has undertaken over the last 20 or so years have spanned the world, from Pakistan and Oman to Brunei and Australia. The scope is large—hundreds of people are currently working in the field and the emphasis is multidisciplinary, with the aim to break down traditional barriers, not only among the different strands of science but also among nations. This is exploration as The Big Picture, preparing blueprints for governments around the globe to work on. For example, the 1977 Mulu (Sarawak) expedition to Borneo was credited with kick-starting the international concern for tropical rain forests.

The society's three current projects include water and soil erosion studies in Nepal, sustainable land use in Jordan, and a study of the Mascarene Plateau in the western Indian Ocean, to develop ideas on how best to conserve ocean resources in the future.

Projects adhere to a strict code of procedure. "The society works only at the invitation of host governments and in close co-operation with local people," explains Winser. "The findings are published in the host countries first, so they can get the benefit. Ours are long-term projects, looking at processes and trends, adding to the sum of existing knowledge, which is what exploration is about."

Exploration has never been more fashionable in England. More people are travelling adventurously on their own account, and the RGS's increasingly younger membership (the average age has dropped in the last 20 years from over 45 to the early 30s) is exploration-literate and able to make the fine distinctions between adventure / extreme / expedition / scientific travel.

Rebecca Stephens, who in 1993 became the first British woman to summit Everest, says she "pops along on Monday evenings to listen to the lectures." These occasions are sociable, informal affairs, where people find themselves talking to such luminaries as explorer Sir Wilfred Thesiger, who attended Haile Selassie's coronation in Ethiopia in 1930, or David Puttnam, who produced the film *Chariots of Fire* and is a vice president of the RGS. Shortly before his death, Lord Hunt was spotted in deep conversation with the singer George Michael.

Summing up the society's enduring appeal, Shane Winser says, "The Royal Geographical Society is synonymous with exploration, which is seen as something brave and exciting. In a sometimes dull, depressing world, the Royal Geographical Society offers a spirit of adventure people are always attracted to."

FURTHER READING

Arnot, F. S. *Garenganze: Or Seven Years Pioneer Mission Work in Central Africa.* London: Hawkins, 1889. Reprint, Cass, 1969.

Axelson, *Portugal and the Scramble for Africa:1875–1891.* Johannesburg, South Africa: Witwatersrand University Press, 1967.

Gerald J. Bender, *Angola Under the Portuguese: The Myth and the Reality.* Berkeley, Calif.: University of California Press, 1978.

Bentley, W. Holman. *Pioneering on the Congo,* 2 volumes. London: Religious Tract Society, 1900. Reprint, New York: Johnson Reprint Corp., 1970.

Broadhead, Susan H. *Historical Dictionary of Angola,* 2d ed. Metuchen, NJ: Scarecrow Press, 1992.

Cadbury, William A. *Labour in Portuguese West Africa.* London: George Routledge, 1910. Reprint Negro Universities Press, 1969.

Chatelain, Heli, ed. *Folk-tales of Angola. Fifty tales, with Ki-Mbundu text, literal English translation, introduction, and notes.* New York, Negro Universities Press, 1969.

Chilcote, Ronald H. ed. *Protest and Resistance in Angola and Brazil.* Comparative Studies. Los Angeles and Berkeley: University of California Press, 1972.

Childs, Gladwyn Murray. *Kinship and Character of the Ovimbundu.* Oxford: Oxford University Press, 1949. Reprint London, Dawsons of Pall Mall, 1969.

Clarence-Smith, Gervase. *The Third Portuguese Empire, 1825–1975.* Manchester, U.K.: Manchester University Press, 1985.

Duffy, James. *Portuguese Africa.* Cambridge, Mass.: Harvard University Press, 1959.

Forbath, Peter. *The River Congo: The discovery, exploration and exploitation of the world's most dramatic river.* New York: Harper & Row, 1977.

Graham, Robert Haldane Carson. *Under Seven Congo Kings, For Thirty-Seven Years a Missionary in Portuguese Congo.* London: Carey Press, 1931.

Henderson, Lawrence W. *Angola: Five Centuries of Conflict.* Ithaca, NY: Cornell University Press, 1979.

Henderson, Lawrence W. *The Church in Angola: A River of Many Currents.* Cleveland, Ohio: Pilgrim Press, 1992.

Hochschild, Adam. *King Leopold's Ghost.* New York: Houghton Mifflin, 1998.

Núñez, Benjamin. *Dictionary of Portuguese-African Civilization, From Ancient Kings to Presidents.* 2 Vols. London: Hans Zell Publishers, 1995–96.

Paul, John. *The Soul Digger or the Life and Times of William Taylor.* Upland, Ind.: Taylor University Press, 1928.

FURTHER READING

Royal Geographical Society. *Journal of the Royal Geographical Society.* "Obituary of Serpa Pinto." No. II, February 1901, pp. 201–02.

Soremekun, Fola. "The Bailundu Revolt," *African Social Research,* 16 December 1973.

Thornton, John K. *The Kingdom of Kongo: Civil War and Transition, 1641–1718.* Madison, Wisc.: Univ. of Wisconsin Press, 1983.

Vansima, Jan. *Kingdoms of the Savanna. A History of Central African States until European Occupation.* Madison, Wisc.: University of Wisconsin Press, 1966.

Wheeler, Douglas L. and René Pélissier. *Angola.* New York: Praeger, 1971. Reprint Westport, Conn.: Greenwood Press, 1978.

ABOUT THE AUTHORS

Dr. Richard E. Leakey is a distinguished paleo-anthropologist and conservationist. He is chairman of the Wildlife Clubs of Kenya Association and the Foundation for the Research into the Origins of Man. He presented the BBC-TV series *The Making of Mankind* (1981) and wrote the accompanying book. His other publications include *People of the Lake* (1979) and *One Life* (1984). Richard Leakey, along with his famous parents, Louis and Mary, was named by *Time* magazine as one of the greatest minds of the twentieth century.

Bruce and Becky Durost Fish are freelance writers and editors who have worked on more than 100 books for children and young adults. They have degrees in history and literature and live on the high desert of Central Oregon. This is their 13th book for Chelsea House.

Deirdre Shields is the author of many articles dealing with contemporary life in Great Britain. Her essays have appeared in *The Times*, *The Daily Telegraph*, *Harpers & Queen*, and *The Field*.

INDEX

Popular Movement for the Liberation of Angola (MPLA)
Central Committee abandons Marxism-Leninism, 132
development of military organizations by, 128, 131
Marxist-Leninist support for, 127–128
officially becomes Marxist-Leninist party, 131
receives assistance from communist countries, 131
Porters, African, 22, *29*, 34, 98. *See also* Carriers
Capelo expedition has lack of, 35
Portugal
African areas controlled by (map), 53
becomes Republic, 111
Britain, as threat to, 99, 104
Catholic Church in
support of Salazar dictatorship by, 42
throughout nineteenth century, 42
causes conflict with Britain, 38–39
colonial policies of, during 1930s and 1940s, 124–125
expands into Angolan interior, 29
extends secular government to control Catholic Church in Angola, 42, 44
free press in, 78, 81
instability in, 120
nationalistic dreams of, 17–18, 38
need for compromises by, 39
offense by European nations to, 33–34
overthrow of monarchy in, 110–111
reaction to news in Luanda, of, 113
pride in African colonies, restored to, 37
search for water passage to Indian Ocean by, 72. *See also* Cão, Diogo
turmoil in, 109–111
and warfare with Ndongo, 72–73
Presidios, 87
function of, 75
revolts in, 76

Press
censorship of, 124
free, 78, 81

Racism, 98
institutionalized, 114–115
regarding schools, 119
under New State, 124
of Serpa Pinto, 36
of some missionaries, 57
Real, Don Miguel, *26*
Republicans, 111
call for Angolan autonomy by, 110
Rhodes, Cecil, 38
Rubber, 21
first-class, 89–90
red, 90
trade
disruption of life due to, 90
dying of, 115
growth of, 98–99

Sabetelu, Jelemia dia, 56
Salazar, António de Oliveira
encourages missionaries to go to Angola, 42
plan for Angola of, 123
positions held by, 123–124
repressive measures of, 127
Salisbury, Lord, 39
San (Bushmen) (1923), *112*
Sanders, William Henry, 46
São Salvador, 69
children (1907), *50*
infirmary (1907), *80*
mission
compound house in (1907), *68*
manual laborers at (1907), *109*
school (1907), *47*
Portuguese garrison in, to protect Dom Pedro V, 55
Reverend Thomas Lewis's description of, 68
Savimbi, Jonas
agrees to act as vice president, 133
agrees to meet dos Santos, 133
heads UNITA, 131
refuses to become vice president, 134
returns UNITA to battlefield, 132
Schindler, T. S., 105
Schools
desire of Department of Native Affairs to make workshops out of, 119

mission, 46, *47*, 116. *See also* Missionaries
conflict with government plans, 119
Portuguese-supported, 51
for training government employees, 113
Serpa Pinto, Major Alexandre Alberto da Rocha, Visconde de
arrogance of, 36, 37
conflict with Britain caused by expedition of, 38–39
description of François Coillard by, 36–37
diplomatic conflict caused by, 37–38
dispute with Capelo and Ivens, of, 35–36
early military career of, 33
exaggerations of, 35, 36, 38
as guest of Silva Porto, 36
illness of, 35–36
joins Capelo expedition, 34
mapping expedition of, 36
meets with Henry Stanley, 35
Ovimbundu assist, 87. *See also* Ovimbundu
racism of, 36. *See also* Racism
receives Founder's Medal from British Royal Geographical Society, 37
return to Europe of, 37
Sertanejos, 23
Serviçais, 98
terrible conditions for, 97, 104
criticism of, 106
Seven Years' War, 87
Silva Porto, António Francisco da, 93
arrival in Luanda of, 19
assists Capelo expedition, 35
becomes government employee, 30
campaigns for Portuguese possession of interior Angola, 26–27
difficult journey of, 25–26
early life of, 18
fading authority of, 15
failing business of, 29
family ties to Ovimbundu of, 23
as intermediary between Europeans and Ovimbundu, 30
marriage of, 23

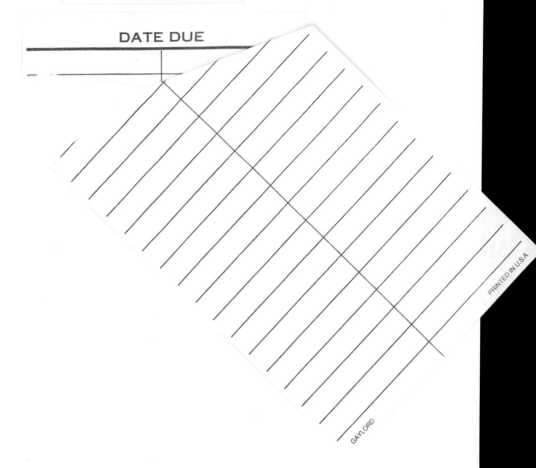

DATE DUE

GAYLORD

PRINTED IN U.S.A.